FACE TO FACE

A deadly drunk driver, a grieving young mother, and their astonishing true story of tragedy and forgiveness

by Audrey Kishline
and Sheryl Maloy

Meredith Books
1716 Locust Street
Des Moines, Iowa 50309–3023
meredithbooks.com

Cover photograph copyright © Chase Jarvis/
Photographer's Choice/Getty Images

Printed in the United States of America.

Library of Congress Control Number: 2007921719
ISBN: 978-0-696-23514-6

Dedication

Sheryl

I dedicate this book in loving memory to Danny and LaShell and to each and every person who has died in such a tragic way before it was their time.

Audrey

To the woman who loves to hear my mother play her favorite song, *White Christmas*, on the piano, and to you, Mom, who stood by me through the worst of times. You were always there for me. I love you and thank you for accepting me for who I am with all my flaws.

Dedication

Table of Contents

1 A Painful Awakening 6

2 The Crash 12

3 From Ballet to Booze 21

4 I Love You 33

5 Not Guilty 37

6 The Funeral 41

7 Guilty as Charged 48

8 Dad's Crash 51

9 House Arrest 56

10 Sentencing 64

11 Starting MM 69

12 Meeting Danny 85

13 MM Meetings 93

14 Facing Demons 102

15 Falling Apart 108

16 LaShell 116

17 Wide-Awake Blackout. 125

18 Unraveling 150

19 Prison 157

20 Beginning to Heal 169

21 Face to Face 172

22 Forgiven 178

23 Getting Back to Normal 186

24 Freedom 191

25 The Nut Farm. 197

26 73 Days 206

27 On My Own 217

28 What Really Killed My Family . . . 225

29 Hello, Sheryl. 226

30 Becoming Whole 234

31 Dateline. 237

32 Face to Face Again 239

    Appendix: 911 Transcripts. 246

    Acknowledgments 256

1 A Painful Awakening

*HI, EVERYONE. I'M LEEZA GIBBONS, AND WELCOME TO
the show. I'd like to introduce you to my first guest. This is Audrey. She
is, I suppose, by anybody's standards a very typical American housewife.
She's the mother of two, and this lady is causing quite a controversy.
Some say what she is doing will kill people; others say she will help save
many lives.*

Leeza, *1995*

March 26, 2000—I awoke in horrible pain. My first sensation was
a violent throbbing in my head. I reached up and felt the bandages
that were wrapped around my neck. There was something clamped
to my face, which I could not actually feel. I was completely numb.
Needles shoved into both arms ran fluids into my body. I could hear
a machine beeping next to me. I could hear the steady "swoosh"
sounds of air being forced into my collapsed lung. My entire body
was horribly bruised and battered. I attempted to focus my eyes
against the sterile white background, but my lids felt like 500-pound
weights and crusty goop and extreme swelling had all but sealed
them shut. The realization slowly sank in that I was in the hospital.

My sisters, Nicole and Tina, flanked either side of the bed,
clutching my cold, clammy hands. They were doing their best to stay
calm as I slowly gained awareness that something was terribly wrong.

"What happened?" I could barely push the words past my cracked
lips and clenched jaw.

And now a controversial alternative to AA—Alcoholics Anonymous.
It's called MM, Moderation Management. There are those who believe
it may be more effective in treating some problem drinkers. And so, in
this morning's edition of "To Your Health" Good Morning America *is*
going to look at the pros and cons of moderation. Audrey, let's start with
you. Do you agree that there is such a thing as a psychologically addicted
chronic drinker who needs abstinence?"

Diane Sawyer—Good Morning America

My sisters had a look of sheer terror in their eyes, and their jaws, strong like mine, were clenched from the tension.

"Did something happen to the truck?"

My sisters exchanged glances across the bed where my broken and bruised body lay. I could tell they were trying to figure out who would find the courage to speak first.

"What happened?" Speaking was nearly impossible. There was something very wrong with my mouth.

"You've been in a car crash, Audrey."

Beep, beep, beep. I could hear the tempo of the heart monitor gaining momentum as dim memories began to take shape.

"Was anyone hurt?"

There was a long pause. The silence was agonizing.

My sisters continued to avoid looking directly into my eyes.

I believe problem drinkers have an option—especially when they look
at their drinking problem early, before it turns into an uncontrollable
addiction. There should be a program that allows problem drinkers to try
to cut back, which most people will try to do before abstaining anyway.

Audrey Kishline—Good Morning America

Total abstinence can be very frightening to some people. Therefore they
delay getting help. We're hoping that moderation programs like the
one started by Audrey Kishline will get people to not only look at their

7

drinking earlier but start doing something about it earlier when their
chances of recovery are much better and before anyone gets hurt.

*Leeza Gibbons—*Leeza Gibbons Live

"Was anybody hurt?" I asked again.

Nicole mustered her strength to speak.

"Two people died, Audrey."

Those words crashed into my brain, and I felt as if a sharp knife were cutting into my chest, slicing away all that had once been my prior life. How? How could I be a fairly normal person one day and wake up the next day to hear I had killed two people? My mind could not absorb the news. I didn't want to believe Nicole, but why would she lie about something so horrific? Her words were unimaginable. Me. I had killed two people.

"I wish I had died too." That was all I could say before I slipped out of consciousness.

The next time I woke, I found my mother and stepfather at my bedside. I had lost a lot of blood at the crash site before being airlifted to Harborview Medical Center in Seattle, about 100 miles away. I had a severe concussion, several broken ribs, and a collapsed lung. And my face—the skin was torn away from nearly half of it, from the side of my nose to the bottom of my chin. Even my tongue was ripped apart. When I arrived I had been taken right into emergency surgery. The massive blood loss had frightened the doctors enough to tell my family to prepare for the worst. The surgeons did what they could to repair my disfigured face, but it was possible, they said, that I would never look the same.

Audrey says, like many people she was a social drinker in her twenties.
But over time her casual beer or two turned excessive, sometimes
drinking up to six or more drinks a day. Fearing for her health and
sanity, she checked herself into a treatment center. Audrey says she
came out of that center branded as an alcoholic. She was told that she is

powerless over alcohol and that she could never drink again. Well, guess what? Eventually she returned to the bottle because of personal problems, this time consuming as much as eight to nine drinks a day. Well, now she says she started getting better when she stopped treating herself like an alcoholic and taught herself how to moderate her drinking. Many say she's in denial. Audrey disagrees.

Leeza Gibbons—Leeza Gibbons Live

My pain medication was administered in such high doses I could catch only small glimpses of reality in tiny, floating pieces. In my drug-induced, dreamlike state, sound bites from the talk shows I had been on promoting Moderation Management bombarded my thoughts. I had started Moderation Management as an alternative support group for drinkers who weren't classified as alcoholics, a program to help teach people how to moderate their drinking and assess if they needed a more extreme program, such as Alcoholics Anonymous. Though it was controversial, I thought I had been making progress in the media showing critics there is an alternative. Now my mind was reeling from the lies, the deceit, the false pretense, and denial in which I had lived for so many years. Whom was I kidding? Looking back, only myself. And now it was too late.

Thanks for having me, Leeza. My program is for people who need to recognize that they're drinking too much. They can make a choice whether they want to reduce their drinking or continue on and most probably encounter problems down the road. If drinking is interfering with your life, if you're drinking daily, starting to have hangovers on a regular basis, not sleeping as well as you used to, and not functioning as well at work, these are signs of having some problems with alcohol. I'm a casual drinker, maybe one or two glasses of wine a night with dinner. I drink because I enjoy it.

Audrey Kishline—Leeza Gibbons Live

On my third day in the hospital, I vaguely recall seeing two people in police uniforms. I knew they were there asking me questions because of what I had done, but at the time it didn't register that I was in big trouble. I was in too much of a fog to remember what they asked me; I doubt I really answered them. My sisters hired James Crowley, a high-powered lawyer out of Seattle, to represent me. He was always present when I was questioned, protecting me when I was in such a haze. I don't think I ever gave a formal statement.

But the reality of what had happened was beginning to come at me in larger, bolder, more threatening slices. My lawyer explained the charges that were being brought against me the first time we met in the hospital. Before that time, in my state of confusion and denial, I actually believed I was going home as soon as I was able. But I wasn't. I was in big trouble. Crowley began to explain the legal process as gently as he could. He never once made me feel bad for what I had done. He did his best to keep me calm and collected. Despite his best efforts, I was in tears almost the entire time I was conscious.

The problem that many people who enter into abstinence-based programs face, Oprah, is that they don't stay abstinent for the rest of their lives. Eventually everyone faces a fall. It doesn't have to be alcohol related. It can be someone who diets. Anytime you deprive yourself of something, it is a setup for failure. You've talked about this on your show many times over the years.
*Audrey Kishline—*The Oprah Winfrey Show

I floated in and out of consciousness for several days after the crash. Every time I opened my eyes, my husband, Brian, was by my side. Brian stands about 6 feet tall and has the most beautiful reddish-auburn hair and beard. He's a big man, with a little extra weight that still makes him look like he's in great shape, so you definitely notice when he's in a room. Even in my condition, even without opening my eyes, I knew when he was there.

Brian and I talked about our love for one another and for our two kids. He didn't want them to see me in such horrible shape, so he never brought them to the hospital. I agreed it would be too traumatic for them.

I knew things were going to be difficult; we were having problems in our marriage prior to the crash, but I knew he still loved me. Despite that, I could see fear and anger in his eyes. I had ruined his life too. But every time I looked into Brian's loving, caring eyes, I promised him things would be different when I got home. Brian tried to reassure me that everything was going to be OK. He told me I had the strength to make it through this nightmare. But he didn't have the heart to tell me that I wouldn't be coming home, not for a very long time.

Other family members came and went during my six-day stay in the hospital. One of my sisters gave me a small, soft tan teddy bear that I clung to and cried into whenever I was awake. I wept and wept, hugging that stuffed bear for dear life. I cried because of pain, but mostly I wept for what I had done. As the morphine was gradually reduced, reality set in. I hurt everywhere, but I knew it was nothing compared to the pain I had inflicted.

"Please, God, if you're really out there, let me die."

2 The Crash

MARCH 25, 2000, WAS A COLD MARCH DAY IN THE YAKIMA Valley in Washington, typical of the weather that time of year. The sun was trying to shine through the clouds, making the snowcapped hilltops glisten. That afternoon and evening I was working as a shift manager at Jack in the Box 45 miles from my home in Yakima. The usual dinnertime bustle of the restaurant was well underway, and for some reason it was unusually busy. We recorded the biggest hour of sales the restaurant had done since Christmas Day. All day long, however, I had a nagging feeling that something bad was going to happen. I was worrying about the safety of my daughter, LaShell. I couldn't shake it. I kept asking myself why I was so consumed with knowing my daughter needed to be rescued. Call it a mother's sixth sense: She knows when her child is in danger.

I clung to the cordless phone all evening, checking to make sure it was working, expecting a call I didn't want to get. At precisely 6:08 p.m. I clearly heard LaShell yell out "MOM!" even though she was 200 miles away with her father, Danny. They were supposed to be on their way home for the weekend. No one else heard the scream, at least no one at the restaurant. But it was as real to me as any voice I've ever heard. I grabbed at the phone and dropped it in a bucket of dish towels. My knees buckled and I sank to the floor.

We were so busy none of my coworkers noticed what had happened before I stood up and regained my composure. I shook it off as fast as I could; I had to regain my concentration on work or risk losing my job. I didn't have time to figure out why I had just fallen to the floor. The restaurant was slammed with orders, so I got busy again, which helped.

Danny was supposed to drop LaShell off at the restaurant around 8 p.m. I anxiously waited for Danny and LaShell to walk through the door, but 8 o'clock came and went with no sign of them. I knew it could take anywhere from two and a half to more than four hours to make the drive, depending on the weather. Perhaps there was heavy traffic, unexpected construction, or unforeseen detours. Plus Danny was habitually late. Maybe he hadn't left work on time, or perhaps he had to make an unexpected stop along the way. Maybe LaShell was hungry and they had stopped for a bite to eat. A dozen possible scenarios crossed my mind as the minutes ticked away and became painful, agonizing hours of waiting.

When my shift finished about 10 p.m., I drove to my parents' house in Grandview, 45 minutes from work. Since our divorce three years earlier, I stayed there on weekends when Danny came home. I was certain he would know to find me there, and I wanted to be with my younger son, Cody, 6, who was already there. My older son, Zack, 14, was staying with friends, so I wasn't as concerned to return home to him. I knew he was OK.

By midnight I still thought Danny would be home soon, so I ate a sandwich and went to bed. I fell into a deep sleep and began to dream. And I saw God. Suddenly there was a white light surrounding Him from every direction. It wasn't a bright light—it was soft, like sunlight pouring through a sheer curtain, shrouding the brightness from hurting my eyes. Then God spoke to me and said, "Just wait. All things will be taken care of in time."

Though I never saw the face of God—it was more of a silhouette—I'm certain He spoke to me once again.

"I told you I would make all things beautiful in my time. Why didn't you wait?"

I answered, "Because I didn't want to."

I woke in a panic. Why did I speak to God that way? It wasn't like me to be so argumentative, especially to God!

Before I could analyze my dream further, I heard a knock at my parents' front door. I jumped up and pulled the bedroom curtains back to see who was there. My heart began to pound. I heard my sister Becki answer the door; then I heard a man's voice asking to speak with my mom. I could hear my sister talking with him, but I couldn't hear everything they were saying. I didn't recognize the voice at first. It turned out to be that of Gary Hughes, a state patrolman and good family friend. His wife had been my sister Becki's elementary school teacher; our families attended the same church.

My first thought was that he was at the house to tell me Zack had gotten into trouble on his skateboard. He and his friends liked to hang out and ride their boards in places the police didn't find appropriate. I figured Trooper Hughes was there to tell me I had to come down to the station to pick up my son.

He began to speak as I walked into the room. I remember hearing him say something about Danny, but in my heart, I already knew he was gone.

"What about LaShell?" I asked.

"She's gone too, Sheryl."

I began screaming and crying. I pounded my fists on my knees, pulled at my hair, and jumped up and down, yelling and screaming, "No. Not my baby girl. No. No. No."

I began to walk in a circle, frantically pacing around the kitchen island, into the living room, and back through the kitchen.

"Not my baby! Not my baby!" I screamed and cried.

I was out of control. Becki and my mother, Norma, called the family doctor to come sedate me. They weren't concerned for my well-being. No, my family wanted to call the doctor because they were so uncomfortable with my emotional meltdown.

None of them had reacted to the news the way I did. There was utter silence from them, and their lack of response was jarring to me.

But my hysterics were intolerable to them. This was a family who covered its pain, who didn't cry or show their feelings.

Becki handed me the phone so I could speak to the doctor myself. I thanked him for his offer to come over but declined to be sedated. I wanted and needed to feel, to experience my pain, sorrow, and grief, to be fully aware of the agony. I had spent my entire life trying to suppress my emotions, but I would not deny myself that right today.

I hung up the phone and turned to my parents.

"How dare you! You have no right to tell me I can't cry! You are not going to rob me of feeling my great loss."

For the first time in my life I realized there was something terribly wrong with my family if they didn't want me to cry over losing my child and my husband. My family stared at me, stunned by my outburst. This was the first time I had ever confronted them over their absence of emotion. Worse yet, they rejected my reason for crying and minimized my insurmountable loss. My baby girl was dead. The father of my children was dead. How could they deny my feelings? How could they be so devoid of emotion?

Cody was sound asleep on the sofa, or so I thought. Only later did he share with me that he actually did wake up that night. He was confused about what had happened and couldn't comprehend the loss. Unaware that he had awakened, Becki moved him to one of the bedrooms to protect him from witnessing my emotional tirade.

By the time I calmed down enough to ask Trooper Hughes some questions, he was gone, so I didn't know any of the details of what had happened. All I knew was that Danny and LaShell were dead. I had so many questions.

I had to pull myself together. My two sons needed me. And though I was physically in the presence of my parents, their cold lack of compassion left me feeling so alone. I lifted my chin, tilted my head back, looked toward heaven, and cried to God, "Now there's nobody who cares about me."

I crumbled to the floor, and once again I heard God speak.

"Yes, there are people who love and care about you." He began to name friends from my Monday morning Bible study class. "They love you. They are whom you must call." His voice was firm but gentle.

I phoned Jeff, my boss from work, who was also a good friend. I got his answering machine.

"Pick up the phone, Jeff! My baby girl's dead!" I slammed the phone down and went into hysterics again.

Next I called my best friend, Sissy. Her machine answered too.

"Sissy, you better pick up the phone because my baby girl is gone." Sissy picked up the receiver. "I'll be right there."

Sissy and I have been friends since we were 15. She's one of those friends who will always be in my life, who has been by my side through thick and thin. I needed her. I needed her comfort and support. She knew me better than anyone and understood that I needed hugs and unconditional support.

Next I called my sister-in-law, Jeannie, with whom I had been very close. All I could say was "Jeannie." It was obvious she already knew because we both started crying before any other words were spoken. She assured me she was on her way.

It was late, nearly 2 o'clock in the morning, or so I thought, but I decided to take a shower. I thought the hot water would help calm me down. I also knew I had a long couple of days ahead of me and wasn't sure when I'd have another chance. I took what felt like the longest shower of my life. I cried and cried as the water flowed over my crouched, naked, vulnerable body. The body that had given birth to LaShell—and now the body that would have to bury her.

I emerged a half hour later, slightly calmer. My father was in the living room sitting in his lounge chair. He was emotionless. I looked at the clock, expecting it to be much later than it was. I looked back at my father and yelled, "How am I supposed to live through three more hours? It's only 3:15. It's supposed to be 6!"

He didn't know what to say. I wasn't making any sense at all. He just gazed at me with his blank stare, completely unable to comfort or console me. He didn't know how to offer any words of hope. If ever I needed the safety and reassurance of my father, this was the night.

As I look back, I realize he must have been as stunned by the tragic circumstances as I was. I'll never know what he was feeling because we've never talked about that night, not ever. I have to believe that witnessing my pain triggered some guilt for his own drunk driving crash so many years earlier. Dad had never seen his family suffer or agonize over his foolish decision to drink and drive. He was too consumed with healing and recovering from his physical wounds to worry about anyone else's emotional scars.

Jeannie and her husband, Randy, arrived at the house shortly after we spoke. My mom and sister went to the Grandview police station to try to gather more information on the crash. I was still waiting for someone to come tell me this was all a terrible mistake. I waited, hoping and praying the news would be different. But it would not change. The truth would not leave. Danny and LaShell were gone.

Jeannie suggested we pick up Zack at his friend's house. I didn't want to go, but it was important that he hear the news from me before he heard it from anyone else. I avoided that daunting task for as long as I could, thinking, "If I never tell him, then it never happened." But I couldn't evade telling my son his father and sister were dead.

It was excruciating to say the words I had to speak that night. I remember holding Zack's teenage hand, a younger yet perfect replica of Danny's. Strong and masculine. As hard as it was, I began to speak, my voice broken, an endless flow of tears streaming down my cheeks.

"I'm sorry, son. There's no easy way to say this. I'm sorry …."

I cried, "I can't do this."

"Yes you can, Sheri," she said.

I sobbed.

"Zackery, your dad and sister are dead." There was no softer way to tell him.

He was silent.

"Can I go back to bed now?" he asked. He was clearly in shock. We all were.

If I let him go back to bed, would he wake in the morning thinking this was all a dream? God, how I wished it were only a dream. My sister–in-law thought it would be best for Zack to come home and be with me and the rest of the family. Even if he didn't know it at the time, he needed his mom. For a moment, for the first time in years, he wasn't a teenager; he was my little boy. We went back to my parents' house so he could rest. I tucked him in, gave him a kiss on his forehead, and made sure he was settled in the room before I let him sleep a while longer. I have never seen my son cry for his loss. Not that night or any night since. It tore me apart. I knew he was in pain too, but he didn't want me to see. He didn't want me to suffer more than I already was.

I never told Cody the news. My mom and Becki broke it to him sometime over the course of the following day. He had some idea something bad had happened, but not until the next day did he know his dad and sister were in heaven.

By early morning my parents' home was overflowing with family and friends who came to offer their condolences and support. All of the questions, hugs, and tears were more than I could bear. Once again I began to cry. Both boys were in the house. My emotional unraveling wasn't helping anyone, but I couldn't stop.

Sissy arrived at the house while I was picking up Zack. She had the *Yakima Herald Republic* newspaper. There was a small story at the top that read, "Man and daughter from Grandview killed by wrong-way driver at 6:08 in the evening."

Up until that moment I hadn't cared much how exactly Danny and LaShell had died. I only dwelled on the fact they were gone, not the reason or the way they were killed. It suddenly occurred to me, however, that the precise moment of impact was when I had collapsed at work the night before. Now I knew why I heard LaShell scream my name.

Shortly after I saw the paper, my mom and sister came back from the police station with more details of the crash. An allegedly drunk driver had killed Danny and LaShell. I became enraged. A drunk driver had taken the father of my children. A drunk driver had taken my precious baby girl. Without Danny, who would I share funny stories about our kids with? Who could possibly understand all the ups and downs we had been through as a couple and as parents? Certainly I could tell these stories to other people, but it would never be the same as sharing them with Danny. Our history died that day. Our family bond was crushed at the hands of a drunk driver.

Newspaper and police reports said that a female driver had been traveling the wrong direction on Interstate 90. I-90 travels east-west and is a main thoroughfare across Washington, cutting through the Cascades. It can sometimes be treacherous, especially in winter. The crash took place on a stretch of the highway known as Snoqualmie Pass. The drunk driver's brown pickup truck pulled out from a wooded shoulder area of the road and began traveling 60 miles per hour heading in the wrong direction. The truck forced several drivers to swerve out of the way, and more than a dozen horrified drivers had phoned the Washington State Patrol to report the reckless driving.

Danny and LaShell were driving behind an SUV, unable to see the oncoming pickup until it was too late. The SUV swerved to avoid hitting the oncoming truck, leaving Danny virtually no time to react. Police later said Danny probably never saw the truck coming. The 1-ton pickup slammed into Danny's silver and blue two-door Dodge.

At first I was told they both died on impact. Months later I learned that LaShell actually didn't die right away. It killed me to learn that LaShell had suffered for any period of time. I was told she died while rescue workers were trying to figure out how to remove her from the crushed car. My daughter had died with no one there to hold her hand or comfort her in her final moments. I don't know how long she was alive, but I was told she was conscious and breathing when the rescuers arrived. If that is true, what was she thinking? What were her last thoughts? I will never know, though I think of it often.

The driver of the pickup was found unconscious, not wearing her seat belt. A half-empty bottle of vodka sat beside her in the front seat. Her blood alcohol registered at .26, three times the legal limit. The identity of the driver, I would later learn, was as grimly ironic as her behavior was tragic. She was Audrey Kishline, the founder of Moderation Management, a self-help movement for people with drinking problems.

3 From Ballet to Booze

I HAVE ALMOST NO MEMORIES OF MY LIFE BEFORE THE second grade. It's probably because my family moved 21 times before I turned 10. We were very poor so my father was constantly looking for cheaper places to live as he bounced from job to job. I called my dad C.R. because he hated being called Daddy, which he thought was a sissy name. C.R. stands for Calvin Richard, his full name. C.R. was practically blind until he was 6 and got his first pair of thick pop-bottle glasses. Although he is not tall, he was very muscular, building an impressive physique with a lot of weight lifting and running. He never went to high school and joined the Army, working in the code department during World War II. He discovered alcohol at age 28 while serving a tour of duty in Germany.

C.R. met my mother in Stuttgart, Germany. Though she was only 15, she was already working as a secretary. My mother was instantly taken with him and thought he was gorgeous. Though he was not a classically handsome man, he had such a charismatic personality, women always wanted to be with him.

Somehow C.R. was able to put himself through college, earning his master's degree in three years while working to support our family. He raised my two younger sisters and me like boys. He taught us that we could do anything that a man could do. Tina was always a tomboy. She loved riding motorcycles and working construction with my dad. Nicole was very feminine, with a beautiful figure.

C.R. loved all of us, but I always felt like I had a special relationship with him that my sisters didn't share. C.R. loved to take me hunting and camping and he taught me to roller skate. None of my friends did things like this with their dads. But there was another side, a darker side, to C.R., which I caught glimpses of.

We hunted for birds, taking our German shepherd with us to help point out prey. In truth the dog was probably too old and sick to be much help, but he was a wonderful companion on those hunting trips. One day C.R. told me the dog had become useless. My dad was raised on a farm with the mentality that animals must be put out of their misery when they become too old, sick, or worthless. He grabbed his shotgun, told me to follow him, and we trekked through the snow to a tree about a hundred yards from our house. The dog stood by the tree; I heard the pop of C.R.'s gun. The dog dropped. I watched as a tiny stream of red flowed over the pure white snow. That was C.R.—empty of emotion and completely unaware of the impact his actions had on me.

When I was 9 my family settled in Boulder, Colorado. C.R. found a job working as the manager of the Highlander Inn Motel, just across the street from the University of Colorado. Our family lived in the apartment above the lobby of the hotel. On weekends the hotel was a place where the college kids liked to hang out and party. The college kids loved C.R. and treated me like their little sister. He made everyone feel welcome. The hotel had a huge swimming pool where C.R. taught us to swim. The pool area was surrounded by a huge concrete courtyard, which felt as big as the university football stadium to me. At night the college kids were welcome to turn the courtyard into a party area. During the day we used it to roller skate. C.R. was an expert skater and he taught me his tricks. I was really good at pivoting, skating forward, then backwards. I loved doing spins.

There were lots of hugs and good times living in Boulder. It was the happiest time of my young life because I felt full of life and very special. C.R. spent so much time with me and my sisters, and I did everything to be a good little girl. I can still hear him telling me to make him proud. I would have done anything to please him.

The good times, however, didn't last long. One night, when I was just getting into bed, my mother came upstairs and said, "Honey, we're going to have to move again."

I was stricken by the news. "But why, Mommy?"

My mother began to cry. I had never seen her break down like that before. She never used the word "divorce" that night. She only told me we were going to a new house, and I was going to get a kitten. I knew something was wrong, but the thought of my own kitten! I was beside myself.

C.R. and his new girlfriend moved to Colorado Springs, a couple of hours away, while we remained in Boulder. The night my mother broke the news, it occurred to me that this move must have been in the works for some time. If my mother had already set up a new home, she must have known this was coming.

Mom never spoke a negative word about C.R. until I was much older. Only then did she tell me the real reason for their divorce. My father was going through a midlife crisis when he met and fell in love with a pretty blonde woman. He came to my mother and said he wanted to be free to be in another relationship. My mother was crushed. She loved C.R., but he wanted an open relationship, which my mother would never accept.

After the divorce my mother had to make the difficult transition from being a stay-at-home mom to working more than 60 hours a week as a secretary just to take care of my sisters and me. C.R. refused to pay any type of child support, but he helped Mom find a house and bought her a car. C.R. left us to fend for ourselves. We rarely heard from him. To me it appeared that we were out of sight and out of mind.

Mother never fought him for money. Having survived the Allied bombings in Nazi Germany, Mom had a fear of the court system. I only remember her going to court once—the day their divorce became final. I had nightmares about that day for years. The dreams were always the same: Mom dressed in the same outfit she wore to court as a big black curtain fell from the sky covering up what once was our family.

Mom's long hours and the demands of her job were taking a toll on her primary role as mother. Her new responsibilities were a difficult change for all of us. In her absence I became a surrogate mother to my sisters. I tried to instill a sense of security and stability, but I was only 9 years old. I didn't know enough to emotionally provide the same way as an adult. Given the circumstances, I did the best I could.

Despite the hardship caused by C.R.'s leaving, I desperately missed him. Not long after he moved away, C.R. moved again, this time to Washington State with his new wife and a stepson. The space between us was now physical as well as emotional. I was crushed when he moved so far away. Every time I saw a car drive by with a man who looked remotely like my dad, I would watch it, hoping it might be C.R., until I was sure it was not. I felt alone and confused. I needed to find an outlet to direct all of my pent-up emotion.

It occurred to me that if my mother was willing to offer me a kitten, I might be able to get something else as well—something I had wanted for a long time, more than anything else in the world. I wanted to learn to dance. As a young girl my mother was enamored with figure skating. She passed on her passion to me, but now as a single mom she couldn't afford the lessons for me. Ballet would be a good, much cheaper substitute. I was thrilled. I dreamt of someday becoming a prima ballerina. My bedroom walls were filled with pictures of professional dancers; my shelves held stacks of ballet books. I daydreamed I was Margot Fonteyn and someday I would dance with Rudolf Nureyev. I worshipped them, staring at them for hours. I desperately wanted to be one of them.

Mom took me to a large dance studio near our home. The instructor was amazed that this was my first time. I had never danced, but I was very limber. I had a slender body that was ideal for ballet.

From a dancer's perspective I started very late. Most ballerinas start out when they're little girls. At 9 I was practically over the hill to be considered seriously. Mom sacrificed a lot to provide private lessons and other training I needed to catch up with the other dancers. I looked at this challenge as an opportunity that would require me to work twice as hard as everyone—which I did.

Ballet was the first time I dove into an activity to erase the pain of something else. As long as I was dancing, I didn't think about C.R.'s absence. Ballet became the next great love of my life.

A few months after we moved from Boulder, my mother began dating Frank. He had been a college student when we lived at the hotel. Even back then he was especially kind and loving to us kids. The relationship between Frank and Mom began to grow, and after about a year they married. I liked him because was loving to my mom and he loved my sisters and me. He certainly made life easier for us.

Shortly after Frank and Mom married in 1967, we moved to New Jersey, where Frank had lined up a good job with Exxon. I was relentless about pursuing ballet. Frank wasn't comfortable with the cost of lessons, so he was relieved when a well-respected teacher agreed to teach me for free. My mother drove me to lessons every day. The drive to and from class became our special time together. I loved that we had developed a close bond and that she was so supportive of this dream we shared.

Frank made a good living, so for the first time in our lives money wasn't a major concern. After seeing how committed I was to ballet, Frank agreed to set up a home studio in the basement of our new house. He put in hardwood floors, a wall-size mirror, practice rails, a stereo, and even a piano. I practiced all the time. Some days I spent anywhere from three to five hours in my rehearsal studio. Ballet was my passion; it was my life.

Although Frank's job didn't require us to move as often as we did with C.R., it did require us to relocate to more distant places. From

New Jersey we moved to Rome, where I enrolled in an international school run by very strict nuns. My dance instructor in New Jersey arranged for me to continue lessons with an acquaintance of hers who taught ballet in Rome. The international ballet corps was a relatively small, close-knit group. If a renowned teacher in one place said a student had promise, other people listened.

School was extremely intense. Academically it was much harder than my school in New Jersey, and I was turned off by the attitude, insincerity, and strictness of the nuns. All I wanted to do was dance, but the ballet school in Rome was lame. I endured a lot of jealousy and ridicule because I was obviously better trained than the other dancers. Being the only American didn't help. I was always relegated to the back of the line. I felt alienated and began to withdraw, growing increasingly depressed.

We lived in Rome for one year. I danced every free moment to hide my pain, to dull the sadness and soften my loneliness. I spent so much time in the rehearsal studio, I often danced until my feet were bleeding and sore. I continued to dance through the physical pain until they didn't hurt anymore. I loved the smell of the hardwood floor in the studio and the feel of the talcum powder on my hands and feet. To me this was home.

When I was 14 Frank's job transferred him to Hamburg, Germany. Once again we moved. I found a teacher who saw greater promise in my dance ability than anyone else had so far. Our new home was in a small village on the southwest outskirts of Hamburg. Frank graciously built another practice room for me, knowing ballet was my heart and soul. My new teacher worked out of the Staatsopern, the city's main opera house, which had a wonderful international reputation for both music and dance.

My mother allowed me to commute alone 90 minutes each way from school to dance and from dance to home so I could study at the Staatsopern. I took the street trolley, which ran from the opera house to the train station, then through some of the roughest neighborhoods in Hamburg. I rarely left the opera house before 9 at night. I was petrified to travel so far alone, but not enough to give up my dream.

I was finally receiving superior training and had opportunities in dance others could only hope for, but the competition was intense. Many of the girls I danced with had started so much younger and had far better training than I did, but I could still outdance them all. That being said, there were areas where my skills were weak, especially in musicality and interpretation. For the first time since I began dancing, I was faced with the prospect of not being good enough.

Once a year the Hamburg ballet hosted an international competition where young dancers were invited from around the globe to dance for two slots on the professional stage. From the hundreds who applied, only 14 were selected for the final phase. I was one of them.

Three months before my family was scheduled to return to America, and shortly after my 15th birthday, I was faced with a critical decision. It appeared that I had a real prospect to turn professional, and opportunities for young dancers were greater in Europe than in America. My maternal grandmother still lived in Stuttgart. Although Stuttgart's opera house did not have the same reputation as Hamburg's, there were several renowned teachers there who all expressed an interest and willingness to take me on. But I wasn't sure I could handle the separation from my family. It had been six years since I lost C.R.; I didn't want to lose my mom and Frank too. Deep down I also harbored a growing fear that I might not have what it took to be successful.

I had been so immersed in the world of dance that I never gave much thought to boys. I always wore my hair back in a ponytail so I never had to fuss with it, and I suffered from bad teenage acne. I wore the same clothes almost every day, as fashion was never a priority. One day, however, a boy who was popular and good looking began to take an interest in me. He had beautiful blond hair and big blue eyes. Every girl in school adored him. Suddenly I didn't want to practice ballet as much, and my feminine self began emerging. I was very attracted to this boy and having feelings I'd never had before. I didn't see it coming, but I became torn between boys and ballet. And it wasn't just boys. It was being a teenager—having a life. I no longer wanted to wake up two hours before dawn and practice ballet before school. I didn't want to leave school an hour early to arrive for practice on time. I wanted to hang out with my friends. I wanted to meet guys. I wanted to go shopping and buy clothes other than tights and leotards. I wanted to be normal.

Dancing was placing some big demands on my life. The instructors constantly berated me for weighing too much. At 5 feet 4 inches, I weighed 102 pounds, yet they insisted I drop to 97 pounds. I was already nothing but muscle and bones and had zero body fat. I wasn't menstruating because I was so thin. But I began dieting in an unhealthy way, not eating enough good food to sustain my health. I lived in extremes. I starved myself, then binged. I wouldn't eat a thing, then I'd stop at a wonderful bakery and scarf down delectable German pastries such as strudel, cheesecakes, chocolate bars, marzipan, doughnuts, whatever I could lay my hands on. At age 15, food—especially sugar—became my next great love.

When my family moved back to New Jersey, I moved with them. By this time my eating habits had worsened. I was bulimic, binging and purging after every meal. I had spent years listening to dance instructors drill into my head thoughts that I was too fat to dance, that I needed to lose weight. The constant berating chipped away at me. I didn't feel good about myself, thin or thinner. Bulimia was weakening my already stressed, frail body. I am thankful that my mother caught the warning signs and began to monitor my eating, at least while I was at home.

Once my eating habits became healthier, however, I made a snap decision to give up ballet for good. It was literally an overnight decision. I wish Mom had tried to talk me out of it, suggesting perhaps that I take a month or two off, but she didn't. Frank, who often referred to me as "Twinkle Toes," was delighted because the tremendous financial burden of lessons would be lifted when I quit. He supported my decision, though he manipulated me into believing it was the right decision for my own good. He explained that the chances of my making it in the small, fiercely competitive world of ballet were slim. He emphasized pursuing a college education. Even so, it took me years to watch other people dance without crying. What had I done?

After I quit I began to gain some much needed weight. I was no longer dancing five hours a day and burning calories faster than I could eat them. I actually got a little chunky. I could see how fat I looked, and it made me feel awful. Once again I was disappointed in myself. That letdown spiraled into a full-blown depression.

I thought a change of scenery might do me some good. I discussed the options with my mom. At the beginning of my sophomore year in high school, we decided I could move across the country to live with C.R.

C.R.—the man who could do no wrong in my eyes. The man who could walk on water.

I don't remember a single phone call or letter from C.R. the years I lived abroad. But I missed him terribly. Children unconditionally love their parents. It didn't matter to me that C.R. hurt my mom or abandoned my sisters and me. I didn't understand the reasons he left until I was much older. All I knew was I missed my dad.

Talking about C.R. in my new family was not encouraged. He broke my mother's heart, and Frank's family only had horrible things to say about him. I always kept my mouth shut. I didn't believe what anyone said about my dad. I knew I would reconnect with him someday. I planned it out in my mind a thousand times. When we finally settled back into our home in New Jersey, I decided to reach out. I tracked down an address and wrote him a letter. I told C.R. that I was having difficulties living with Frank, and I wanted to come spend some time with him. In my teenage mind going to live with C.R. was more exciting than staying in suburban New Jersey.

C.R. responded to my letter by calling to say I could come out to see him.

"No problem!" he said in a loud, happy voice, as if we had never been apart. I was thrilled. I packed my bags and headed west.

By that time C.R. was the principal of the high school in White Salmon, Washington. He was also working construction on the side with the grand hope of becoming the biggest construction firm in the state. C.R. always had a good work ethic. He was filled with big hopes and dreams and always instilled the belief in me that I could do anything. He did a tremendous job building up my shattered self-confidence. He always told me how smart I was and never put an emphasis on appearance.

School was a breeze. The academic standards in White Salmon weren't nearly as tough as my schooling in Europe. Plus C.R. wanted to bring me into his world. He taught me to shoot guns, which was a big deal for him. He lined up empty beer cans on a tree stump, handed me the gun, and taught me how to pick them off one by one. He taught me how to line up the gun, aim, hold my breath, and then release it, exhaling slowly as I pulled the trigger. He also showed me how to use a bow and arrow. I wasn't that great at bow hunting, but I loved learning things most girls my age never dreamed of. It was fun, and I got to spend a lot of quality time with C.R.—something I very much wanted.

I began working construction with C.R. too. He taught me how to run an 8-ton crane. Eventually I was so good at it I was able to work large jobs on my own. I became one of the guys. I dressed like one and looked like one. I loved it. Construction was the antithesis of ballet. Compared to the rigors of dance, construction was a cinch. As far as I was concerned, life was really good. I was happy and fulfilled and doing something that once again tapped my passion.

On the job C.R. treated me like any other member of his crew. I was just 17, but I was experienced and willing to do whatever he told me. I was beginning to feel confident again, especially when my coworkers bragged about the little girl who operated their crane with such precision and finesse. I loved the camaraderie of being on a site and the freedom, so different from the strict rules back home while I was dancing. I was out in the real world, loving every minute.

After work C.R., his crew, and I would head out for drinks. The routine was basically the same every day. I either worked the crane or mixed and poured concrete. As soon as the whistle blew indicating it was the end of another work day, I'd jump into C.R.'s big pickup truck and head down to the corner store for a six-pack of beer that C.R. and I always drank on the way home.

"Work hard, play hard," that's what C.R. always said. A six-pack after work became a normal part of my daily life. My entire life with him I had witnessed C.R. drink nightly after work. He was what is often referred to as a "maintenance drinker." C.R. measured his intake not by the glass but by control. He never got roaring drunk in public, never lost a job over alcohol, never caused a fatal accident, and never started his day out with a drink. In C.R.'s house this translated into someone who has control over alcohol. Drinking did not have control over him. That was the logic on which I was raised.

Drinking, then driving was never an issue for C.R. either. After a hard day's work, my dad would stick his hand out and expect me to place a freshly cracked-open can of beer in it for him. He always drove on the back roads and never lost control. For C.R. that was what it was all about. Control. His drinking never appeared excessive. To me that was normal drinking. C.R. cautioned me that if my drinking affected work the next day, I had a problem. He talked about people we knew in common who were problem drinkers, alcoholics. He pointed out their behavior, being clear to say they were killing themselves with alcohol. C.R. warned me that I didn't want to ever be one of "those" types of drinkers.

I will never forget the first day I drank with C.R. It was a few days after I arrived in White Salmon. I had sipped a few drinks before—a taste of champagne on New Year's Eve or a little beer, especially when I lived in Germany—but never to the point of feeling the effects of alcohol. C.R., Jane, and I were in the living room of their house. We opened a couple of cans of beer. It was very cold and it tasted good. It gave me a euphoric sensation. Everything seemed brighter and looked and sounded different. I think I drank an entire six-pack myself that first time. I felt our conversation was so connected and deep. I had a whole new perspective on life. I loved everything about the feeling I got from drinking. More than anything I had ever loved before or since, I loved it. Alcohol become my one true love.

I graduated as my high school valedictorian. Like most kids I went off to college, but school just didn't hold my interest. By now I knew I had to feel passionate to stick with something. I dropped half my classes and looked for something new to pique my interest. C.R. had always loved to fly. I thought it might be something I could be interested in too. I started taking lessons and was hooked. I wanted to become a commercial pilot, so I quit school, moved back in with C.R., continued working construction to earn extra money, and started training for my commercial pilot's license.

And I drank every day.

Sheryl

4 I Love You

AT THE TIME OF THE CRASH, DANNY AND I HAD BEEN
divorced about four years following 12 years of marriage. Despite
the divorce we were still trying to work on our relationship to see
if there was a chance we could find a way to put our marriage back
together. Although we both dated other people over the years, I
was still very much in love with Danny. I didn't tell anyone in my
immediate family we were trying to work things out. I was fearful
that they would interfere with our relationship as they had done
so many times in the past. I was careful not to let anyone influence
Danny or turn him against me. One of the biggest problems we had
as a couple was our lack of communication skills and our inability to
understand each other's perspective. I know in my heart that we both
tried the best we could, and there certainly was no lack of love—only
a lack of knowledge on how to make our relationship work.

Several months before the crash, around August 1999, we
decided to reconcile, but we were taking things slowly to make
sure we didn't hurt the children if we weren't able to get completely
back on track. We had moved beyond the anger that had developed
toward the end of our marriage. Since I had forgiven Danny for all
of the arguments and disagreements, I knew in my heart I wanted
to let go of the anger too.

Later that year, in an attempt to pay down the debts I had
accumulated as a single mom, I went back to work at a Jack in the
Box in Grandview as the night shift manager. I wanted to have all

of my bills paid off before any reconciliation so no one could accuse me of getting back with Danny because I was in a financial tangle. I was already filled with so much doubt and anxiety about how other people might perceive Danny and me reconnecting.

Danny worked as an electrician on a temporary job in Bellevue, near Seattle, during the week and drove the three-hour trip back to Grandview on the weekends to be with the kids and me. I couldn't work the night shift on weekdays because there was no one to watch the kids, so I had to put my hours in on the days and nights Danny was home. Sadly, he misinterpreted my night shifts as a way of avoiding him and not working on our relationship. His frustration began to build until it came to a breaking point that Christmas Eve.

My boss gave me Christmas Eve off so I could be with my family, with the understanding that I would have to work on Christmas Day. Danny was terribly upset at the thought of all of us not being together for the holiday. The old anger boiled up and turned into a fight.

"Admit it. Admit that you hate me," I yelled as I stood in front of him at our home on Cedar Street in Grandview.

Danny would not respond.

"I hate you!" I didn't mean it, but those were the words that poured from my mouth. I grabbed the children, packed up the car, and drove to my mom and dad's house on the other side of town.

I went to work the next day, and Danny went back to work in Bellevue for the week, planning to come back to celebrate New Year's with his family. We both continued to say we were determined to work through our problems. But we never found the time to sit down and talk about what happened that night. Three months passed in silence while we pretended everything was fine. I didn't have time to break down or the desire to nurture Danny's constant insecurity. I had a job and a family to take care of, and that's where I was focusing 100 percent of my energy and attention.

My birthday came and went in January without any

acknowledgment from Danny, which broke my heart. A few weeks later on Valentine's Day, I suggested we meet together to talk about our future. Danny was still seeing another woman, but I believed he wanted to make things work as much as I did, maybe just not as fast. I kept praying about our relationship for months. In my heart, in the very deepest part of my soul, I wanted my family back. I wanted our family to be whole again.

It was clear that we had to make significant changes if we were going to give our relationship a fair chance. For starters, we would have to move away from the negative history in Grandview. A new environment would give us a fresh start and be good for everyone. LaShell went to Bellevue with her dad for the first time in late January to see if she liked it and to assess whether her brothers would do well there. I couldn't make the trip because of my hectic work schedule, but I trusted LaShell. Even though she was not quite 12, she had good natural instincts. If she liked it, I'd know it was the right move.

LaShell and I loved spending time together, going to the movies or out to lunch, spending lots of girl time together. We had the exact same taste in clothes, so I knew if I bought something I loved, I had better buy two because LaShell would want one of whatever I brought home. I missed her every time she was away for a few days, whether at Danny's or having a sleepover at a friend's.

The weekend before LaShell's 12th birthday, which was March 15, she and I were in the kitchen washing dishes. I often called her my "baby girl," though I knew she was growing up fast.

"Mom!" she said that night. "I'm almost 12 years old now. I'm going to be 13 next year. I am not a baby. Quit calling me your baby girl."

I just smiled and said, "LaShell. You will always be my baby girl. I will always love you—even after you die."

I stood in the kitchen, oddly aware of what I had just said. "Even after you die." Why did I say that? Why in the world did those words slip out? They hung in the air for some time in that awkward silence that night. None of us could possibly foresee their meaning.

On the afternoon of March 25, 2000, I received a call from LaShell. She had accidentally locked herself out of Danny's camper in Bellevue. My maternal alarm went off. I can't explain it, but I felt an uncontrollable urge to rescue my baby girl, even though she was several hours away. Something inside me knew LaShell needed to be saved that day. LaShell was cold and scared, but I assured her everything would be fine and that she and I would go out for hot chocolate when she arrived home. I called Danny to tell him to go home immediately and unlock the door.

We spoke for a few minutes and decided we would talk when he brought LaShell back later that night. We both agreed it was time we made some decisions about our future. As excited as I was to finally clear the air with Danny, every ounce of my being wanted to tell him not to come—that he should spend the night in Bellevue. I had a premonition something bad was going to happen. But if I told him not to come, I knew he would think I didn't want to see him. Even though it was March, I kept hearing the song "Blue Christmas" in my head. I knew I would have a blue Christmas later that year if I let them make the trip. But it wasn't my decision, and I said nothing. I didn't know where these thoughts were coming from—nor did I want to dwell on them. I had to be at work in a few minutes, so I had to put those thoughts out of my mind and keep convincing myself everything would be fine.

Danny told me he'd be at the restaurant by 8 o'clock. I said, "I love you, Danny," as I hung up the phone. Those were the last words I spoke to him.

Audrey

5 Not Guilty

I WAS IN THE HOSPITAL FOR SIX DAYS UNTIL MY
attorney arranged to have me moved to an alcohol treatment center.
He purposely had me sent to Springbrook Northwest in Newberg,
Oregon, because it was far away from my home in Washington. No
one could know where I was—not even the judge. This is the usual
course of action because it allows lawyers to work through the details
of a case while their clients safely dry out. I was ordered by the court
to remain in that treatment center for the initial period of formal
arrest and arraignment until I received my court date in two to three
weeks. The intention was to give me a place to recover from the worst
of my injuries before I faced a trial or had to go to jail.

I was still in a tremendous amount of pain when I was admitted
to the center, but they immediately took me off my pain medication.
My entire body ached. I couldn't breathe in too deeply because of
my cracked ribs, and my mouth and tongue hurt from the stitches.
Eating was very hard because I could barely close my mouth and
food spilled out everywhere. I was still dizzy all the time from my
head having hit the steering wheel so hard, and I had a bad case of
vertigo, which lasted for months.

I was at the center almost three months. It was my first
experience of being held somewhere against my will. The detox
process was minimal because I was already detoxed from my
hospital stay. Every day consisted of having my vital signs checked,
going to alcohol awareness classes, group therapy sessions, mock

AA meetings, and forced "fun" time, which included playing games and drawing pictures.

The living conditions at Springbrook actually were rather nice. It was an expensive treatment center that catered to wealthier patients. But I always felt under constant pressure because of my pending prison time, trying to process killing two people, missing my kids, and having to do everything perfectly during treatment or face being tossed out of the program. If I was kicked out of Springbrook, I would be sent directly to jail, and I knew I wasn't ready for that life yet.

After my first three weeks, I was allowed to go to Seattle for one day to see my attorney, James Crowley. Brian took time off work to drive me the four hours each way for the meeting to start talking strategy for my case. My hotshot attorney was a flamboyant, gregarious, in-your-face kind of guy who looked a little like Fabio. He had long hair pulled back in a ponytail and he was always dressed to the nines. He was expensive, more expensive than I could afford. Brian and I had just spent our last dime on our new house, the first house we bought during our 13 years of marriage. The medical bills already threatened to take the house; the legal bills were just beginning. Knowing our financial situation, my aunt offered to pay for Crowley's legal services.

Although my lawyer knew my story, he truly believed prison was not the right solution for me. Deep down I think he understood it was pretty rough inside and I might not be tough enough to make it through. Initially he encouraged me to plead not guilty. He explained to me it was standard procedure. Doing so would give him time to build my defense or plea-bargain with the prosecutor. He created various scenarios where he was able to convince me he could get me off without doing any prison time. He said that since I had been taking antidepressant medication perhaps I had had a bad reaction to the pills, which in turn could have caused me to be disoriented. He also told me the police did an illegal search of my truck, which he could use as a technicality to have the charges dropped. He even thought perhaps there was ice on the road that spun me around, causing me to crash into the oncoming car. He kept giving me plausible scenarios, though none of them were the truth. He told me how he had just gotten off a client with four DUIs who had also killed two people. He wanted to hire a private investigator and look into every possible loophole.

Despite the truth and against my better judgment, I did what almost anyone would do. I took my lawyer's advice and pleaded not guilty.

But, of course, I *was guilty.*

It didn't take the news media long to pick up on the story of my crash. The headlines screamed, "Founder of Moderation Management Kills Two People Drunk Driving." Nearly a week after the crash—my second night in the treatment center—I was still the lead story on the evening news. My photo was digitally imposed on the car I had struck. The tangle of metal was unrecognizable, far too small to ever have been a car. That image was another large dose of reality. Looking at the image on television, I realized that I had caused that—me and my foolish drinking.

One day during rehab I received an envelope in the mail with a return address I did not recognize. I had no idea who it could be from—very few people even knew where I was. I barely knew where I was. I opened the letter and two photographs fell to the ground. They were pictures of a young man and a pretty blonde-haired girl— Danny and LaShell.

I knew I had killed two innocent people. I was fully aware of what I had done, yet I couldn't remember the victims' names. For whatever reason I just couldn't retain that information in my head. At first I thought it might be a side effect from my concussion. Later I realized my subconscious blocked it all out. Up until the moment I opened the envelope, the crash was like hearing a news report about a soldier dying in some far away country. I knew I had killed a little girl and her father. I felt sad but not emotionally connected because I didn't know them. How could I feel pain and sorrow for two people I had never met? They were nameless, faceless strangers. The depth of my crime didn't sink in until I saw those photos.

I began to read the letter.

"May God Bless You."

I was stunned to read such kind words.

My knees buckled and I fell to the ground crying.

I held the picture of Danny, who was so handsome, and LaShell, who looked to be around the same age as my own daughter. These were the people I had killed. Danny and LaShell. Names and faces.

From that moment I have never forgotten their names and faces.

"I'm guilty. You know I'm guilty. We have to change my plea."

I confessed the obvious truth to my lawyer, knowing he would try to talk me out of changing my plea. I knew I could never live the rest of my life denying what I had done. You can't kill two people driving drunk and expect to get off without paying the consequences. I had to make things right. I could have chosen to make excuses and look for loopholes, but that would have been like my decision to drink and drive. What kind of example would I be setting for my children if I didn't own up to what I had done? And I knew the victims' family was out there too. Even though I hadn't connected with any of them yet, I understood that my actions had hurt them well beyond my own pain. I owed it to them to take responsibility. Even if I didn't remember committing the crime—I would do the time.

6 The Funeral

RESCUERS WORKED MORE THAN SIX HOURS TO REMOVE
Danny and LaShell from their crumpled vehicle. The entire front
end of the car was smashed like an accordion, with the front seat
pushed into the trunk section of the car. I wasn't allowed to see
Danny's body; his injuries were so severe the coroner refused to
let me see him. I insisted on seeing LaShell. Seeing her would be
excruciating, I knew, but I still needed to see her with my own eyes.

My sister-in-law Debbie took me to view LaShell's body at
Smith Funeral Home in Sunnyside, about eight miles from my
home. The funeral director escorted Debbie and me to the morgue.
One of the owners of the funeral home who was quite close with
my grandparents approached me and asked, "Honey, what are you
doing here?"

She was unaware that the little girl on the table was my daughter.
I pointed to the room we were about to enter. She turned white as
she realized the body on the table was LaShell. She hadn't recognized
my baby girl; LaShell was so grown up since the last time she had
seen her.

I was escorted into the small room where LaShell lay. I was
unprepared to see her so suddenly in such a stark place. The reality
that the lifeless body on the table in this cold room was my baby
girl smacked me in the face, and I lunged forward to hold her.
Debbie put her arm out to stop me. The funeral director had made
it clear I wasn't supposed to touch the body because she hadn't been

embalmed. But I so desperately wanted to hug her and hold her, kiss her forehead, and make all this go away. I wanted to whisper in her ear that everything would be all right. I wanted to pick her up off that cold table and carry her home to take care of her. I kept quietly telling LaShell, "You're going to be OK. Oh, baby girl, baby girl. Why did this have to happen?"

LaShell looked peaceful. Beautiful. The funeral home had tried to conceal the severity of her injuries. Originally I was told the car didn't combust on impact, but I later found out it had. LaShell's face was red from flash burns caused when the car ignited. The intense heat had burned her face as if she had stayed out in the sun too long—only worse. I shuddered to think of the terrible pain she must have felt.

I could also see a big gash on her forehead. "You always had to bust open your forehead, didn't you, baby girl?" The crash was the third time in her young life she had cut open her forehead.

The first time it happened she was 2 years old and we were enjoying a family lunch on a hot summer day. LaShell was running all around the house, happy and playful. I warned her to slow down or she might hurt herself, and sure enough, she crashed right into the bookcase in our entryway and cut open her forehead. Danny and I took her to the hospital where they stitched her up with five butterfly stitches to avoid scarring.

The second time was later that fall when we walked to meet Zack at the school bus stop one afternoon. LaShell saw a bug on the sidewalk and bent down to check it out, but she lost her balance, fell, and cracked open that same spot. Once again the doctors had to stitch up my baby girl. The crash had opened the same gash for a third time. This time there would be no stitches to fix her boo-boo. This was an "owie" I couldn't fix.

Before we left the funeral home, the funeral director handed me a bag she said contained Danny's clothes. She told me they were wet. I never looked at them. I never opened the bag. His pants, shirt, bright yellow fleece vest, and shoes all had been cut off his body. His wallet and cell phone were missing. The funeral director pointed to a large drawer in the corner of the morgue and said, "Danny is in there." It was the coldest, eeriest feeling I have ever had as I pictured him in a big green garbage bag, crumpled up like an old newspaper.

The thought of Danny in that drawer put me over the edge. "Get me out of here," I said to Debbie.

For several days after the crash, I called Danny's cell phone, letting it ring and ring, hoping to hear his voice. I wished he could come home and help me handle the daunting task ahead. Danny was stronger than I was. He was the head of our household. Despite our arguing and disagreements, he was always there for me when I needed him. He could be gruff at times, but he could handle tough situations. That's what I needed most at the moment, but I had to handle this one on my own.

Both the boys understood that Danny and LaShell were in heaven. I think for them the hardest part of losing their dad and sister was watching their mother suffer. They couldn't stand to see me in such pain. Thank goodness children have the ability to bounce back from tragedy and trauma. The day after the crash Cody and I were in the truck on our way home from my in-laws, and I began to cry again.

Cody threw his hands in the air and asked, "How long is this going to go on, Mom?" He sounded just like Danny, who throughout the years had difficulties with my emotions. I had to laugh. I needed to laugh. Any levity was good, even at my own expense.

The memorial service for Danny and LaShell took place on March 31, on a beautiful sunny day with not a cloud in the bright blue sky. The day of the service, I got up and began getting the boys ready. I checked on the flowers and all the arrangements for the gathering that was to follow the service.

My dad was standing at the front door of the Nazarene church in Grandview. He was standing there with his brother-in-law, my Uncle Bill, and his best friend, Russ. Dad hugged me and sobbed—a first for me to see. Uncle Bill had to pry my father away so they could begin the service. I had never seen my dad express such emotion until the funeral. It caught me off guard. I didn't know how to react to his sadness. To this day he still cries when we talk about LaShell.

The service was exactly as I thought Danny and LaShell would have wanted it. I fought to keep it simple and dignified. At the end of the service, Zack and I had to go forward to receive an American flag that was presented to us by the local chapter of the VFW because Danny had served in the military for eight years. We took it together, our hands reaching out, as if it were the last piece of Danny we would ever hold.

Danny wasn't coming home. I could hope, wish, pray, and plead with God to change things, but the reality began to sink in that I was all alone. Since the bodies were not viewable, I chose to cremate both Danny and LaShell. I talked to both my boys and we all agreed. Zack didn't want the ashes in the house; he said it would be too spooky for him. I drove with the urns seat-belted in the front seat of my truck until the burial.

A month after the memorial service, Cody stopped playing outside. He had always been an active boy, the kind of 5-year-old who moved a hundred miles an hour until he exhausted himself. Then he'd reenergize his batteries and start all over again. After the crash, however, Cody just sat around, playing for hours with his Legos and watching television all day long. He picked at his food and retreated into a quiet, lonely, sad world. I tried talking to him about how he was feeling, but I usually received answers through shrugs of his shoulders and one-syllable words.

"Cody, why don't you want to go outside and play? What's the matter with you?" I turned off the television and waited for an answer.

He continued staring into the blank screen, never letting his dark brown eyes look up to see me standing there.

"Cody, I want an answer."

He needed to get back to doing little boy things for his own peace of mind.

Still staring straight ahead, he answered, "I can't go out and play because I lost my best friend."

My heart broke. I hadn't thought of his loss like that. His sadness was so different from mine. Cody climbed up and snuggled with me on the couch. For the first time since the crash, I understood his emptiness and loneliness for his sister.

Zack had an equally hard time adjusting to our new life. He had been very close with Danny. He became physically sick from dealing with his grief, and I feared losing him too. Zack couldn't deal with the pressure of school or with the attention being thrust on our family because of the crash. I agreed to homeschool him until he felt ready to go back to high school.

None of us was prepared for the media frenzy that followed the crash. Newspapers, television stations, and radio shows called the house all the time wanting to hear my feelings about Audrey Kishline, the Moderation Management founder turned drunk driver, and about losing my husband and daughter. I spoke to whoever called, though I have no recollection of what I said. I remember feeling numb, shell-shocked. No matter how often I spoke about the crash, my reaction was always the same. When the interview was over, I felt empty, alone, lost, and scared. My single message was clear: Don't drink and drive. (In fact I still have those words recorded at the end of my voice mail greeting.)

Most of the TV shows did a pretty good job telling the story, though I marveled at their ability to stay detached when the interviews ended.

I finally stopped answering the phone when a Seattle television station tried to set up an intentional confrontation between Audrey and me. They encouraged me to agree to the meeting by suggesting I could scream, cry, curse, become as mad as I wanted. They wanted me to tell her off, as long as their cameras were there to record the exchange. All they wanted was evil. It would never happen. Never.

On July 17, 2000, which also happened to be Danny's birthday, the television show *Inside Edition* did a story in which they took some family members and me to the crash site for the first time. The show made arrangements for the highway patrolman who had been first on scene to meet us there. Interstate traffic was diverted while the patrolman escorted us and the newscaster around the site. I was shown where Audrey's truck spun around and finally struck the metal barrier. The officer showed me the skid marks, still visible, deep enough that the asphalt was creased from the skidding tires.

The producers didn't want me to go with them to film Danny's car, which was being stored at the State Patrol impound in Ellensburg. I was told it was too morbid. But I was adamant. I wanted to see the car. I wanted to face it head on, in person, and get it over with.

The highway patrolman explained what had happened to Danny's car in the crash; how both the front and rear seats had been pushed into the trunk. I had no idea what that meant until I saw what had been Danny's Dodge two-door, now less than 6 feet long. The sight made me sick. The patrolman wept—twice.

After seeing the wreckage of the crash, driving became really hard for me. For the first few weeks, I didn't drive at all. But I had two young boys to care for and driving was essential. I didn't want to end up like my mom, who has never driven a car and is dependent on someone else to drive her places. So I got back behind the wheel when Zack needed to see a doctor and there was no one to take us. I had to psych myself up every time because I was so fearful of oncoming cars. I've since gotten over that, but every now and then my fear comes back.

It didn't seem like six months had passed when we decided to bury Danny and LaShell in late October. They are buried in Prosser Cemetery, in Prosser, Washington, close to the house we lived in. Danny and LaShell are buried next to each other on a grassy plot near a couple of benches where I can sit when I visit. The day of the burial, I bought a bunch of colored balloons for everyone to let go into the sky as we buried Danny and LaShell. I did this as a way to celebrate their lives and so we could send them something special in heaven. Since then, whenever Cody gets a balloon, he lets it go so his sister and dad know he's thinking of them and that he loves them.

Burying Danny and LaShell brought me a sense of closure I hadn't yet felt. Their ashes finally had a home where the boys and I could visit whenever we wanted.

Audrey

7 Guilty as Charged

"MRS. KISHLINE, ARE YOU AWARE OF THE CRIMES YOU ARE being charged with today?" The judge addressed me directly.

"Yes, your honor."

"And how do you plead? "

"Guilty, your honor."

I was *very* guilty.

The judge found me guilty of two counts of vehicular homicide. He didn't say much, but his carefully chosen words made it painfully clear he detested me for my crime. I was given one month on house arrest to set my affairs in order before my sentence would be handed down on August 11.

I rose from my chair inside the Kittitas County Court in Ellensburg, Washington, bracing myself for the next step—something I was dreading but knew I had to do. Because of the media attention on my case, I had agreed to hold a 15-minute press conference where I would read a prepared statement and the press could fire away with questions they had about the crash. I hung my head low; I didn't want to make eye contact with anyone. I glanced up for a moment and caught a glimpse of a dark-haired woman standing at the back of the crowd that had gathered inside the courtroom. I don't know why my attention was drawn to her; she was just another face in the crowd. Yet I couldn't take my eyes off of her. And then it hit me: This was no bystander. She was Sheryl Maloy Davis. The thought had never crossed my mind that she would be there.

I swallowed hard as the reality of who she was set in. She was younger than I expected, a mother, just like me, and yet we were so different. I still had my daughter; she did not. If someone had run over my daughter, my first reaction would be total anger: Let the judge throw the book at the person who took the life of my baby, and I would live bitter and miserable the rest of my life. I had destroyed this woman's world, and my shame and guilt were as intolerable as my crime was unforgivable.

The media had been in relentless pursuit of me to grant an interview and describe what had happened the night of the crash. I agreed to the press conference so I could answer their questions once and never have to face the press again. I didn't want anything to do with giving interviews. I wanted to go to court, tell the judge I committed this disturbing crime, and get it over with as fast as possible. My sudden change in plea had stunned the waiting press. I hope it came as a relief to many, but I just wanted to apologize to Sheryl and her family. I wanted to apologize to MM. There was so much to say, and yet it all boiled down to two tiny words.

"I'm sorry."

Two simple words I didn't have a chance to say to Sheryl in the courtroom that day.

The press conference was held on a grassy area behind the courthouse. Brian sat stoically beside me as I read my statement. There were a sea of reporters and a bank of microphones in front of me. I don't remember my exact words that day, but I know I tried to express my sorrow. I wanted Sheryl and her family to know that I wished I could bring back their loved ones. I took responsibility for what I had done.

After I finished my statement, reporters rapidly shouted questions at me. I did the best I could to answer each one without looking up. As I spoke, my thoughts wandered to Sheryl, wondering how she was handling the mayhem. She had been thrust into the media spotlight amid the loss of her family. I could only imagine how hard for her it must have been. I worried that all of the focus on me would somehow detract from the depth of her feelings. My pain was terrible, but hers was unimaginable.

In my heart, I wanted to scream and shout, beat my hands against my chest, and cry out, "I'm sorry." But those words felt so inadequate. They would never bring Sheryl's daughter back into her arms.

When I finally could look up, I saw pain in so many people's eyes. I was once again drawn to Sheryl, who was now flanked by two men I hadn't noticed before. One appeared angry. Something in Sheryl's eyes spoke to me, perhaps the pale, tight expression on her face. Seeing her that day reinforced my decision to plead guilty. I had nothing left to hide. I was raw and exposed, emotionally naked.

When the press conference was over, Brian took me back to our house, where I would remain under house arrest for the next month, awaiting sentencing. The truth hit me hard when I arrived home and was forced to place an electronic monitor around my ankle. A special technician came to the house with the bracelet and installed a breath analyzer with a camera attached. I would be required to submit to frequent, random breath tests during my arrest. I was in my home but already felt like I was in prison.

Brian was quiet at first. There wasn't much to say. I think he understood I needed some time to deal with what was happening. He held my hand and hugged me tight. He was solid as a rock, trying his best to protect me from the inevitable.

8 Dad's Crash

I WASN'T SURE WHY AUDREY CHANGED HER PLEA. AT the time, I had to believe she did it to avoid negative publicity as the founder of Moderation Management. It had taken me a few months to move past Audrey's original plea of not guilty. I sat in the back of the courtroom that day in total disbelief that this woman could say she was not guilty. Her lawyer originally argued that she had no memory of the incident, and despite her blood alcohol level of almost three times the legal limit, she could not be held liable or accountable for taking two innocent lives. Her toxicology report also showed high levels of antianxiety medication and antidepressants, both medications that come with firm warnings against consuming alcohol while prescribed.

I had tried to shield my family for months from the media, which endlessly covered the crash and Audrey's pending trial. When Audrey changed her plea in July, that meant there would be no need for a trial. The judge would sentence her and that would be that. I was grateful not to have lawyers debating the details and circumstances of the crash. No one would have to testify. There would only be a hearing and sentencing. It was a tremendous relief.

Even without a trial, recounting the moments that Danny and LaShell were killed had opened up some old wounds, ones that reached all the way back into my childhood, ones I hadn't thought about for a long time. It had been just a few years ago that I realized the reason my family didn't celebrate New Year's Eve until recently.

My family's way of coping with tragedy has always been to simply pretend it didn't happen, but I couldn't do that now.

When I was in the second grade, my family lived in Frankfurt, Germany. Dad was in the Army, so as a military family, we had a tendency to move around a lot when I was growing up. It wasn't unusual for my dad to be gone for days, weeks, and sometimes years at a time (while serving in Vietnam), leaving his wife and kids so he could do his duty.

My dad also had a long history of drinking, so there were lots of times when he didn't come home after a hard night of partying with his Army pals. There was nothing special about this particular New Year's Eve, 1972—especially when Mom and I went to bed without the chance to wish Dad a happy New Year. Like so many nights before, he was out for the evening.

A few hours after going to bed, I awoke to find my mother pacing back and forth across the family room of our small apartment. She was worried—and waiting. I joined her, following her like a shadow back and forth across the room. I could feel her (and my own) panic building, though I had no idea why. I was too young to allow my thoughts to go where my mom's already were.

Four days passed with increasing tension before we got the knock on our door that changed our lives. It came from one of my mom and dad's good friends who lived downstairs. He came to tell us that Dad had been in a horrible accident and his prognosis wasn't good. Allegedly he drove his car off the Autobahn, flying down a 300-foot drop-off. The crash shoved his body partially through the windshield, then back in again when the car came to a stop on the hillside. My dad's best friend and drinking buddy was with him that night and was thrown several feet from the car, fracturing his pelvic bone. We knew him well. It wasn't unusual for him to come to our apartment for dinner, to babysit us kids, and sometimes to crash on our sofa. His injuries, however, were minor in comparison to the permanent, devastating effect the crash had on my dad.

They ruled it an accident, but looking back I know it had been only a matter of time before Dad ruined other people's lives with his frequent decision to drink and drive. This was no accident. It was an inevitable event.

After hearing the news, Mom frantically found a way to the military hospital in Frankfurt where Dad had been taken. She paced there too, something she would do for weeks after the crash. Dad was forced to lie in bed for a good part of his nearly 12-month recovery. He had suffered a broken arm, a broken leg, and had severe internal injuries. His arm never healed from the extreme break and he still wears a leg brace. The first time I was allowed to see my dad, he was in a full body cast that covered everything except his left arm.

Alcohol-related crashes have marked several other important transitions in my life. Dad's crash was the first, and until Danny and LaShell were killed, the most powerful. I have defined my life as BC (before Dad's crash) and AC (after crash). Before Dad's crash he was very much a part of my life, and the memories of my family were filled with laughter and fun. There might have been some problems, but we still connected as a family.

Many years before, Dad had served two and a half tours fighting in Vietnam. I don't have many memories of him then. It wasn't until we moved to Germany that he began having any sort of presence in his children's lives. I remember how Dad used to take me to the corner store with him in my pajamas and snow boots. He used to play with all us kids—sledding, teaching us to ride our bikes, and other fun stuff. He bought me a big purple bike with a banana seat when I was still too small to ride it. It had training wheels on it, and I hardly ever rode it unless Dad was around to help cheer me on.

I cherished every moment we had before the crash. But for me, growing up stopped in the second grade. I went from innocent child to jaded victim the night Dad crashed his car.

As the oldest of four children, I've always felt like the caretaker for my younger brother and two sisters. I was only 7 years old and just a few years separated each of us, yet I bore the brunt of the responsibility of taking care of them on a regular basis.

My family never openly talked about Dad's crash. The bits and pieces I know come from sporadic conversations with my mother over the years. It was too hard for everyone to discuss. Like so many other difficult things that happened in my family, there was no acknowledgment that this tragedy even occurred.

Desperate for help with my siblings and me, my mother moved us back to Washington State. When I left Germany, I didn't know if I'd ever see Dad again. Three months after the crash, his condition had stabilized enough to relocate him to a VA Hospital outside Washington, D.C. But he might as well have been in Germany—to me, he was a million miles a way.

To add to the intensity of his crash, just before the incident my mother discovered my dad was cheating on her. For years my dad believed he was the bad guy—that he screwed things up the night he crashed his car. He never knew that Mom had her secrets too.

My mom and I had never had a good relationship. It had always been strained. Dad didn't know my mother was physically and verbally abusing me. I remember sitting on my parents' bed the day my mother found Dad's photo of his mistress in his dresser drawer. Mom took the photo out of the drawer, turned to me, and began to scream and yell at me as if it were my fault. She beat me because my dad had a girlfriend. In my mother's eyes, my knowledge of Dad's affair coupled with being the victim of her abuse made me a horrible threat to her. Throughout the years she became increasingly abusive toward me, and to this day the effects of that abuse continue to impact my life.

My pain and angst grew and deepened. By age 8, I knew too many things little girls should not know or understand. As I grew older my mother accused me of being a bad girl, a slut, and worse—you name it. She believed that's who I was and said so, as if she were trying to convince me. Eventually I started to believe what my mother was saying and tried to live down to her expectations. In the eighth grade I tried drugs and alcohol because in my mind that was who my mother had taught me to be. I smoked cigarettes, I snuck out of the house at night, and I partied with my friends.

As I got older, however, I didn't want it to be that way; I didn't want to be her scapegoat anymore. I tried to talk to her to make her understand that, but she didn't listen. Her response was to beat me. Her perspective was that I deserved to be abused. I grew to believe she might have been abused as a child too, and that helped me make sense of how she could have done what she did.

When Dad came home from the hospital about a year later, he was a complete stranger. He looked and sounded different and was distant and caustic. He took out his bitterness and anger on me and my siblings. He began beating me too, perhaps to appease my mother, who nagged away at him about how terrible I was. But we never talked about things like that; they just happened and we went on.

I did have one relative I could trust. My mom's mother, Grandma Margaret, was a wonderful lady who died of cancer when I was 13. Grandma Margaret was loving and warm—everything a grandma should be. She was the only woman in my young life who ever showed me compassion and unconditional love.

Through all the rest, I learned to guard myself and developed a tough exterior. On the inside, though, I was tainted by those years, and I felt my family didn't want me to be happy. It seemed they would do anything to prevent me from having love and joy in my life.

Somehow I knew my parents' image of me wasn't who I really was. I realized my mother's accusations were wrong, and it became my mission to prove it. I stopped all of my misguided ways and turned back to God. I have since forgiven all of those involved in my abuse and have been able to move beyond their hurtful ways. I choose not to dwell on that time in my life.

9 House Arrest

BECAUSE OF MY ANKLE MONITOR, I COULD TRAVEL ONLY in a tight radius around the confines of my home. Even walking to the mailbox was beyond my limits. If the bracelet went out of bounds or I attempted to cut it off, I would immediately be taken to jail. I was also required to take random automated breath analyzer tests five to 15 times a day. Each time the analyzer, which was connected to my home telephone system, took my photo and sent it real time, like an email attachment, as I blew into the machine to verify to the monitoring station I was the person being tested.

Being home brought up so many bad memories. All of the good memories were mysteriously erased. The stress level in the house was at an all-time high, especially between Brian and me. We could barely talk about the reality of what had happened, let alone the future. I hadn't yet figured out how to tell the children what was happening, but sooner or later they would need to hear the truth. Lindsey was 11, old enough to know something was going on. Samuel was only 8. I worried they would somehow find out what I did from someone else before I had the chance to explain it myself.

I had been away three months during my treatment, but it must have felt like a lifetime. I am thankful Brian was home to take care of the children. He was working at a small software company near our house. If he couldn't be home to meet the kids after school, his mom or stepdad, who lived nearby, took them to their house.

Our house was in Woodinville, Washington. It was not that attractive on the outside—a single-level, gray house with a flat roof, like a typical manufactured home. It was in a wooded neighborhood that had everything from moss-covered metal trailers to million-dollar homes. We loved to take long walks up and down our road looking at the strange mixture of homes.

We knew we only had a short time left together as a family, and no one knew how long I would be gone. I spent hours pacing back and forth outside on the deck, smoking cigarettes, and drinking cups of coffee. I was fixated on how much time the judge would give me. I knew I deserved the worst, but I had to pray for the best. I spent as much time as I could outside, soaking in the sun, the fresh air, and the sounds, smells, and flavors of summer. I watched the kids play in the yard and ride their bikes up and down the street behind our house. Sometimes I forgot my circumstances, but those moments were few and far between.

I already felt like a prisoner, like a leashed animal. I couldn't stand being in this horrible state of mind. Everything reminded me of the dark days that had led me to this place. Worse yet, I could see the hurt I had caused Brian and the kids. I tried to put on a happy face, to laugh and be normal, but underneath the surface lurked the awful truth.

My attorney warned me the judge was especially furious about my case. The fact that I had written a book on alcohol awareness and was viewed as an expert on the subject escalated his ire. I was well aware the judge was not alone in his opinion. The thought of the prison sentence he would hand down terrified me. I had heard horror stories from AA members who had served time. I felt like it was a real possibility that I would die in prison; I wasn't a strong enough woman to survive that type of environment. I was a suburban housewife who would soon find herself surrounded by hardened criminals.

I desperately wanted to drink. It was the only way I knew to dull my pain and calm my anxiety. It had always been my medication of choice whenever I felt my life was spiraling out of control. Going through this sober made me crave drinking even more.

I spent my last 30 days of freedom divided between my role as mother and wife and my identity as an addict. I couldn't look at Lindsey and Samuel without wondering what life would be like for them when I was gone. My heart was thick and heavy with the thought of my two beautiful children growing up without their mother. How would Lindsey and Samuel cope with losing me for years? I didn't want to live without them, and I didn't want them growing up without me.

Samuel played and laughed in the backyard unaware of what was happening. I sat on the back porch and smiled as he innocently embraced every moment. I hadn't the heart to tell him Mommy was going to leave again. I spent afternoons and evenings reading to Lindsey, who had inherited my love of books, and watching her lip-sync and dance to her favorite songs. Every chance we had, I wanted her to feel love and joy, peace and security. My heart split in half, filled with both love and utter sadness every time I looked at them.

It was clear that Lindsey knew something was going on, and I often found our roles reversed. Lindsey nurtured me when she could tell I was down. She brushed my hair, stroking my head and assuring me everything would be all right. She was seeking love and attention—two things I'm sure were absent when I was drinking. As the waiting stretched out, I could see Lindsey going through a transformation, as if she understood that soon she was going to be the lady of the house, the one taking care of Daddy and Samuel.

Still, days passed and I hadn't found enough courage to tell my kids the truth. My sleep was restless, if I slept at all. I wasn't eating and was losing weight at an alarming pound or more a day. The resulting high level of ketones in my blood threw off my daily Breathalyzer tests. Every so often when I breathed into the monitoring machine, it tested positive for alcohol. The police were instantly notified and were at my house within minutes. I had to beg them to believe me that I had not touched a drop of alcohol since the crash. Each time this happened, I was rushed to the local police station to be retested on a more sophisticated machine. The analysis always came back with a zero blood alcohol level, but my already heightened state of panic intensified with every test for fear of repeating this horribly embarrassing cycle.

I became manic, going through extreme highs and lows. Sometimes I ran around the house, talking fast, trying to organize all our paperwork and necessary documents. At other times I was almost catatonic. I closed the curtains and lay in bed for hours in the dark. I usually called Brian's mom to come pick up the kids for fear they would see me in this condition. My personal levees broke wide open, and I was drowning in an emotional flood of guilt, shame, and remorse. I felt like all the years of hiding and suppressing my emotions were crashing down on me like a tidal wave that just kept coming and coming. I thought it would never end.

August 11, 2000, loomed. My sentencing date was less than a week away. I had to tell my children what happened. There was no easy way to break the news to Lindsey and Samuel that their mom was a drunk and an addict who had killed two innocent people.

The story was still all over the news and front pages of the newspapers. The media attention on my case was a blessing and a curse. On one hand I hoped my story would make people think twice before making the same mistake of drinking and driving. On the other hand it produced a great deal of stress for my family, as well as Sheryl's family and everyone connected with Moderation Management. For years I had lied about my life. Now everyone knew that I was a liar. Even me.

As hard as this would be, it was time to start telling the truth. I took Samuel and Lindsey by the hands and sat them down at the table. The three of us sat quietly for a moment. Fighting tears and trying not to let my voice crack with the struggle of getting the right words out, I began to speak.

"A few months ago, I made a big mistake. I got very drunk and drove our car into another car on the freeway. Two people died. A little girl your age, Lindsey, and her father."

I saw Samuel's big blue eyes widen. I could tell he didn't have the capacity to really absorb all that I was saying. He was only 8 years old—much too young to take it all in. Tears began rolling down Lindsey's face as I explained I was going away for a little while. I was honest—I admitted what I had done and that I was now suffering the consequences of my poor choices that had brought me to this place. Telling my kids that I killed two people and trying to explain how something like that happened to their mommy was excruciating. I couldn't bear to see the pain on their faces as it slowly soaked in that their mom was going to be gone. Lindsey would be driving by the time I got out, and Samuel would no longer be a boy—he would be a teenager.

Brian did what he could to support me during this challenging time in our lives, but I'm certain he had mixed feelings.

I knew he still loved me, but he was also in a lot of pain and shock. We had been together for 14 years. What was he going to do? How could he work and take on the roles of both a mom and dad all on his own? That last week we spent as much time together as we could. We drank our coffee together in the morning, sitting on our couch looking out the windows into our backyard filled with beautiful tall fir trees. We tried to act like everything was normal, keeping things as simple as we could under the circumstances. But we knew our relationship was falling apart under the pressure.

Our lawyer had advised us that we should start divorce proceedings before a wrongful death civil suit was filed against me. We could be sued for millions of dollars, he said, even though we didn't have that kind of money to pay, but a divorce could help protect Brian from financial ruin and perhaps salvage some security for my children's future.

The day of my sentencing arrived. Oh, how I dreaded this day.

Strangely, the warm, sunny day felt far too nice to be the day I went to jail. I dressed in the only expensive, professional black suit I owned, a suit I bought when I was doing the talk show circuit promoting MM and my book. I thought maybe the judge would take pity on me if I looked nice. I asked Brian to stop for a latte on the way, a privilege I would soon be denied. My husband, mother, stepfather, brother, and two sisters accompanied me to court. Brian and I dropped the kids off at his brother's house on the way. I hugged my children longer than usual in those moments, but I refused to cry. They turned to walk into the house, and I watched the door close behind them. I closed my eyes to hold on to every feature of their young, innocent faces. I told Brian to pull away slowly so I could cherish the moment for as long as possible. I didn't know when I would see them again, but I was sure it wouldn't be soon enough. I looked out the car window, watching Samuel wave goodbye, and they were out of sight. Oh, my God. They were gone.

I smoked several cigarettes outside the courthouse in Ellensburg in anticipation of what the judge would deem as a fit sentence for my crime. My thoughts were overwhelmed by my countless fears of what prison would be like, how the guards would treat me, and what endless hours in a cell would feel like. I was filled with angst and had nothing to help me numb it. As I walked up the courthouse steps, I felt as if I were walking the plank, knowing I was about to free-fall into the ocean to my death.

My attorney had told me I would be allowed to make a brief statement. I looked at this as my last opportunity to formally address what I had done. I worked on my statement longer than any other speech I had ever given, but it seemed all I could utter were a few brief sentences:

"There is no way to explain how sorry I feel over what I have done. I do not ask for leniency. I just want to make it very clear that I am deeply sorry."

I wasn't apologizing just to Sheryl. No, that statement was a blanket meant to cover all of the people I had hurt. Every person in my life was deeply wounded by my mistakes.

At the sentencing only the distance between the two tables at the front of the courtroom where I stood with my lawyer and Sheryl stood with hers separated us—we were less than three feet apart. I could see every detail of her face and eyes, especially as they teared up.

She had come to court with an army of support, and the judge allowed several of them to speak. As they read their statements, the extent of the damage I had caused pounded deeper and deeper.

The judge asked Sheryl if she wanted to make a statement. She began to speak, her words becoming muffled as my head fogged over from thoughts of her pain and suffering. The only thing I remember hearing Sheryl describe was her daughter's blonde hair. Thoughts of Lindsey drove home the painful truth that I had taken the life of someone else's child. I will never forgive myself. Never.

The judge asked me to stand. His cold eyes told me he was angry. As he read his statement, I felt the walls closing in on me fast. He made it clear I was just another drunk who had caused so much devastation.

"I am going to give you the absolute maximum sentence I can. I only wish I could give you more."

I stood motionless. I knew I didn't deserve leniency. I held my breath waiting for the judge to continue.

"You are going to be in the system for a very long time."

He paused long enough that I began to shake and cry.

"I hereby sentence you to four and a half years."

Four and a half years was just a number when I heard it. I went numb.

"I wish I could give you more time," the judge repeated.

Those words crushed me, but he was right. How much time is enough for killing two people?

With the fall of his gavel, I went from living a fairly normal, middle-class life as Audrey Kishline—wife, mother, sister, daughter, tennis-and-swimming-lesson mom, gardener, and cook—to murderer, felon, inmate, and convict. Nothing more, nothing less.

I was allowed to hug my mom and dad, who had been in the courtroom for every painful second of the case. To my surprise, some friends of Sheryl's approached me and said nice things as they hugged me. Each of them spoke of Jesus' love for me and his understanding and ability to forgive all sin. How could they even stand to touch me?

Two guards placed handcuffs around my wrists and led me through a large metal door. I had no idea what waited for me on the other side.

10 Sentencing

FIVE MONTHS HAD PASSED SINCE THE CRASH. THE DAY of the sentencing was fast approaching. Most of the media were relegated to the hallway outside the courtroom, but a few stations were allowed to film the proceedings. I was far more concerned with representing my family, especially Danny and LaShell, than I was with how I might look to the media that day. I was still a mass of tangled emotions, but my grief had come and gone. Life was moving on. Friends and supporters were around at first, but now the phone hardly rang and people rarely dropped by to see how I was doing. Life was moving on. I thought Audrey's sentencing was the last chapter in this long and draining nightmare, and I just wanted this day to be done.

I arrived at court flanked by family and friends who were all there to see justice served. My brother-in-law Bill told me the judge might not let the family make any statements because he was afraid they would be too repetitious. I think the media presence was another concern. I insisted I have the opportunity to have my say. It was an important element in my healing. I was the only voice Danny and LaShell had. Since they were unable to speak for themselves, someone had to speak on their behalf. The prosecutor told Bill he would do the best he could to try to secure us a chance, but he made no promises.

I can't remember the exact order of who spoke when, but I remember listening to Audrey's stepfather beg the judge for leniency for his daughter. He asked the judge to consider her two children at home who needed their mother. All I could think was how this mother had taken the life of my child. What about my kids? My sons needed their dad too. I also vividly recall Audrey as she began to speak. She cried as the words "I'm sorry" quietly slipped from her quivering lips.

Before her sentencing the judge asked if anyone wanted to address the court. The judge set a strict time limit so no one could ramble. Bill and his wife, Debbie, spoke before me. I remember Bill's words clearly: "You must take this woman, this menace to society, and lock her up and put her away where she belongs."

I can't recall what Debbie said, only that she was quite emotional. And then it was my turn.

I found myself unable to say everything I had intended. I spoke of LaShell—what a loving and caring person she was. I described her beautiful sparkly blue eyes and silky blonde curly hair that glistened in the sunlight. I told the courtroom how she had the perfect touch of pink in her cheeks that brought out the effervescent red in her lips. She was so beautiful, so perfect.

I spoke about how much she loved her brothers. She was the apple of little Cody's eye, and she adored and idolized her big brother, Zackery. I told the court I didn't want to share any personal, cherished moments I had with my baby girl because I didn't think anyone there deserved the privilege.

"I will never be able to hear about my baby girl's first kiss or see her walk down the aisle at her wedding. I will never know how it feels to see her graduate or become a mother. I'll never hear her say, 'I love you, Mom,' again. I will never feel her hug or smell her like I did when she was still my baby girl."

I talked about Danny's perfect clam chowder. I asked how my boys were supposed to grow up without their dad. It was so painful to talk about losing two people so close to me at the same time. Oh, how I longed for him to be there with me, not in heaven looking down.

As the judge began his sentencing, he spoke with authority. He did not find Audrey's story moving or justifiable. He angrily voiced his opinion on the crime that had been committed. I remember him telling Audrey she was a menace to society. He pointed out that he wanted to give her a life sentence. He made it clear to her that if he could have, had there been a precedent allowing him to do so, he would have sent her to prison for the rest of her life. Although he sentenced Audrey to serve the maximum years possible by law, it was only four and a half years for each death. In his own words it was "not enough time" for the crime committed. The judge declared Audrey would serve her sentences concurrently, following the plea agreement to which the prosecutor had agreed. My heart sank.

I looked up at the judge and wanted to scream, "Your honor, out of curiosity, which of my loved ones is the 'freebie'?" I was livid but remained silent.

After sentencing, the judge turned to me and my family one last time and said, "If you don't want people to get away with murder, then you must use this case to speak up and be heard to get the laws changed." I realized he was saying I had the power to change things so other families would never have to endure the pain I was feeling. I couldn't sit at home wasting away in my grief. I had to become an advocate to prevent others from making the same mistake Audrey had—and if they did, I wanted to be certain they paid dearly for their misguided decisions.

I left the courtroom through a set of large double doors that separated the entrance to the hallway. "Is this all there is?" I kept asking myself. I couldn't believe it was over. I walked through the cold, sterile white hallway of the courthouse corridor. It seemed endless—and empty. "I'm all alone" was my single thought. Nobody was there. Just me. Alone. All alone.

It didn't fit. Where was everybody?

The flash of a camera brought me back to reality. I was in fact surrounded by people, reporters, friends, family, loved ones. Yes, I was alone, metaphorically, yet hundreds of people surrounded me, shouting out, asking questions.

"Sheryl, how does it feel?"

"Do you think justice was served?"

"Do you agree with the sentence?"

I caught sight of Kristy, a friend of mine from church, off in a corner crying by herself. I made my way through the sea of strangers trying to pry their way into my most heartbreaking moment. I walked over and asked Kristy, "What's wrong?"

"I'm so sorry. I didn't know this was going to affect me so hard."

I hugged my friend and told her everything would be OK.

My sister-in-law Jeannie was with me when I turned around, still surrounded by cameras and microphones. I wanted to leave. I had to get out of there.

After Audrey's sentencing, my attorney began to push for filing a civil suit. He described how I could go after Audrey's family assets, their home, Brian's business, everything. But they didn't have any assets to go after. Furthermore Brian was threatening to divorce Audrey as a protective measure in case I tried to seize anything. I wasn't out to punish or hurt anyone, especially her children. They hadn't done anything wrong and had already been hurt enough. I was seeking something far greater than money. I was looking for peace.

After the crash I searched my Bible every day looking for answers and guidance. Many verses helped provide comfort and ease the pain I felt. But one message seemed to repeat itself over and over from the pages.

"Do not judge and you will not be judged. Do not condemn and you will not be condemned. Forgive and you will be forgiven." The words from Luke 6:37 seemed to jump out every time I read. As a Christian, I wanted to represent Jesus Christ in all my actions and words. With God's guidance, I also knew I wanted to show my children the proper way to live. The Bible's message was clear: I had to forgive Audrey.

For several months after the crash, however, forgiveness was merely a word. If I were going to forgive Audrey for her sins, my action had to have meaning. It had to be backed with pure intention and done with God in mind and heart.

I wanted to be certain that going to Audrey and telling her face to face, "I forgive you," was exactly what God wanted me to do. I didn't want to be like the Pharisees who bragged, "Oh, look what I did." It had to be purely God's will. It had to be sincere, real, and true.

My hesitancy wasn't in doubting God's wishes. It was in overcoming what other people were telling me. Even my closest friends couldn't accept my need to forgive the woman who had killed my daughter and Danny.

The week Danny and LaShell were killed, my Bible study group had been reading Psalms 11, which says, "In the Lord I put my trust. How say ye to my soul, flee as a bird to your mountain? For lo, the wicked bend their bow. They make ready their arrow upon the string that they may privily shoot at the upright in heart. If the foundations be destroyed, what can the righteous do?"

People were telling me I should be home, crying. I knew that wasn't what God wanted for me. I knew He would protect me from anything people would say or do to harm me or deter me from following what was in my heart.

I spent hours devoted to private prayer time and became deeply involved in my church and Bible study group. I found great comfort in the company of others who could embrace the road of forgiveness I was following. This time of seeking to draw God closer helped cleanse my mind and heart and soothe the rawness of my wounds. The pain I felt when I came across a pair of Danny's shoes or one of LaShell's T-shirts—small reminders of the family we once were— did not go away, but it was slowly subsiding.

I knew what I had to do. I was comforted by my decision even if it made others squirm.

11 Starting MM

I STARTED DRINKING DAILY IN MY EARLY 20s. EVERY evening I drank one, two, even three glasses of wine, sometimes more. Before I met my husband, Brian, I liked to party on the weekend, especially during the years I worked in construction. I thought that was a normal life. In my 20s I dated a man who worked in the hotel business. Our lives revolved around entertaining clients and patrons, which usually meant late nights and lots of booze. Most of the people I associated with were heavy drinkers too. Fun and good times meant alcohol was involved.

Alcohol also became a way to cope with life—the ups, the downs, and the in-betweens. I drank when I was happy, when I was sad, when I was bored, and when I didn't know how I was feeling. I didn't need a reason to drink, but I always found one. Mostly I drank because it was a habit—a bad habit that, looking back, was beginning to cause problems in my life. I didn't feel well and didn't eat right, and I slept poorly when I slept at all. The amounts I drank gradually increased, and the hangovers became more frequent and severe. I began having difficulties keeping up with courses I was taking at night school in Santa Barbara and later when I lived in Ft. Worth, Texas. I started to postpone everything—studying, projects, hobbies, even socializing with people I knew didn't drink as much as I did. I often drank irresponsibly, risking other people's lives when I drove after I drank too much. Finally, after my first long-term relationship fell apart, I started to drink alone. Still, at the time, I didn't see what alcohol was doing to my life. I didn't know any other lifestyle with which to compare.

Then I met Brian in January 1985 at a bar in Seattle where a lot of people went after work on Friday afternoons. He had just returned from a software engineering job in Saudi Arabia. I was impressed with Brian because he was such a gentleman. He came from a good, solid Italian family and represented everything I wanted in creating my own family. I wasn't hiding my drinking from him—I had no reason to. It didn't seem abnormal, at first.

After spending time with Brian, however, I began to recognize that excessive drinking wasn't normal. It wasn't the way everyone lived. Most of all, it wasn't how Brian lived.

Brian was always romantic, often bringing me flowers and doing little things that made me feel special. I had never been in a relationship with someone like Brian. He was centered and directed. I knew I was truly in love with him after a particular date in Seattle. It was just before he was to leave for a job in Ohio that would separate us for several months. We went out for pizza, something we did at least once a week. I sat across from him, looked into his honest, loving eyes, and I just knew I was in love. There was a moment that night when I understood that Brian knew me from the inside out. He understood me better than anyone ever has before, and he genuinely loved me.

I became depressed after Brian left on his job. I was lonely and couldn't believe how much I missed him. In his absence I began drinking to an extreme again and often woke up hungover. Both of my sisters had successfully beaten their addiction to alcohol. Nicole quit drinking in her early 20s through AA and a treatment center. Tina simply quit in her early 20s, though like me she would never label herself as an alcoholic. Both were living productive lives in recovery. I was inspired by their successes and aspired to follow in their footsteps toward living a sober life. I decided to go to a treatment center for help. Probably my greatest motivation was that I loved Brian so much I feared losing him if I didn't clean up my act. I knew I had to quit drinking if we were going to make things work. It was time to seek help.

My impression of those who checked themselves into an alcohol treatment center was they were generally drinking significantly more than I was. I didn't want to be labeled an alcoholic. The word terrified me. I knew that once you're labeled an alcoholic, you are always considered to be an alcoholic. I felt as if I had a permanent scarlet letter "A" on my forehead that stood for "alcoholic." In my mind that meant I could be nothing else. Going to treatment was an extreme choice given what I thought of as my consumption habits, but I was willing to do whatever it took so I wouldn't lose the man I loved. I envisioned the treatment center filled with people who woke up in the morning, poured themselves a drink, and continued drinking throughout their day and into the night. In my mind these were people C.R. used to warn me about as a kid. They lost everything: their jobs, family, friends, all of the things I still had in my life. I hadn't lost a thing—not yet anyway.

I wrote Brian to tell him I had checked myself into an alcohol treatment center in Yakima, Washington. I told him how I had taken the bus to C.R.'s house in Colville and had spoken to a local counselor, who helped me make the decision to check myself into the center. I remember clearly how I wrote the words "I'm an alcoholic" on the page. It was a hard admission.

Brian wrote me back to offer his love and support. In fact he wrote me letters every day I was in the center, and he came to see me. He told me he was surprised by my decision to seek help, that he never noticed I had a problem with my drinking. We had been on lots of dates, drinking wine together, but he said it had never occurred to him my drinking was out of control.

Nearly 10 years later, when I wrote my book *Moderate Drinking*, I defined an alcoholic as a chronic, severely dependent drinker. Other definitions of alcoholic might include any person with any type of drinking problem, including moderate levels of alcohol-related problems. At the time none of those described how I saw myself or my drinking. I simply felt I needed help to quit consuming alcohol. I never saw it as a chronic problem in my life. Never.

After treatment and with my new alcoholic label, I had a clear idea of what a traditional alcohol treatment program was like and I didn't care for the experience one bit. My "disease" was treated through a 28-day inpatient program on the third floor of a hospital. This particular program was run by two little old ladies, both former addicts, with little training for rehabilitation. The center was a small building in the middle of the desert, housing only 12 patients. I attended group psychotherapy, received confrontation counseling, and learned life skills training. I had to perform therapeutic duties such as making beds and cleaning bathrooms and was ordered to take daily vitamins. My detoxification consisted of sleeping in a room separated from the rest of the patients where a nurse took my blood pressure and temperature regularly for 24 hours. That was it. I experienced no significant withdrawal symptoms, which indicated to me that my physical dependence on alcohol was not all that severe. I spent my free time sunbathing, smoking cigarettes, and drinking coffee. That was all there was to do in that place.

The experience also introduced me to an institutionalized version of Alcoholics Anonymous, which forced me to attend meetings on a daily basis. I use the term "institutionalized" because these meetings were held in the treatment center. I say I was forced because I was informed that if I did not comply, I would not graduate from the program. If I didn't complete the program, my medical insurance would not cover the nearly $25,000 cost of my treatment. In order to practice the steps of the AA program, I was told to fill out workbooks based on the treatment center's interpretation of the first five steps of AA's 12-step program: admit I was powerless over alcohol, admit I was not sane, turn my will and my life over to the care of God, write a moral inventory, and confess my wrongs to God.

Spiritual training was another aspect of the treatment I received for my supposed medical disease.

In my AA meetings I was simply known as Audrey, an alcoholic. To me the label never seemed to fit. I was uncomfortable every time I heard the word, let alone used it to describe who I was. It became the definition of my whole being, and I hated it. I would have been so much more comfortable in AA meetings if I could have said something like "My name is Audrey, and I'm an individual who has a drinking problem." Or "My name is Audrey, and I want to change my life." Or "My name is Audrey, and I want to live better and drink less." Any of those would have been better than "My name is Audrey, and I'm an alcoholic."

Treatment center personnel repeatedly emphasized that I would have to attend AA meetings for the rest of my life. And if I didn't? A dire prediction was that I would end up dead, in jail, insane, or in the gutter. My family was told the same thing in meetings they attended as a part of my recovery. With this kind of warning, I should have made sure that I went to meetings for several years after inpatient care. But their description wasn't the path I saw myself on. No. I faked my way through treatment, sitting through the meetings bored out of my mind because I still didn't see myself as a true alcoholic. I didn't recognize that I needed to be in a program like AA.

After completing treatment, I went to Ft. Worth to be with Brian. I tried to stay sober, but I slipped again. I binged for two straight days. I checked myself into another treatment center, which wasn't much better than the program in Yakima. I spent the next several months trying to pull my life together and working on my relationship with Brian.

After a year of dating, Brian proposed to me. In an expensive restaurant in Ft. Worth he got down on one knee, held out a ring, and popped the question. We married in 1986 in a small ceremony at the justice of the peace. His mother wanted us to have a larger wedding so family and friends could help celebrate our union, so on July 11, 1987, we had a second wedding in Seattle. It appeared as though I had gotten my life back on track and that alcohol was no longer an issue. Things were going really well in Brian's career too. Even though his job required us to travel all over the country, living in no fewer than 10 states in the first nine years of marriage, we were happy.

I gave birth to our daughter, Lindsey, in 1989, and to our son, Samuel, in 1992. Giving birth and seeing your baby for the first time is astonishing. They open their eyes and have this incredible moment of clarity. They look right in your face, and in an instant everything is different. When Lindsey was born, I was completely overjoyed. Brian and I had conceived once before but were forced to abort the pregnancy because the baby was extremely malformed and would not have lived, even if I had been able to carry to term, which the doctors doubted. I was 32 years old, and the pregnancy was considered to be high risk. I was devastated. For three months after losing the baby, I could do nothing but cry. So to have two healthy children after that was miraculous.

With each city Brian and I moved to, I sporadically attended AA meetings. I became thoroughly familiar with the AA program throughout the early years of our marriage. I met wonderful, warm, genuine, caring, and sincere people at every meeting. But I must admit I didn't really relate to their stories or the severity of drinking, and I certainly never felt like going to an AA meeting was like coming "home," a phrase I heard often but couldn't grasp. Although in the beginning I tried desperately to belong, I never really did.

There were times during those first years of marriage when I'd fall off the wagon, sometimes drinking all day until Brian came home from work to find me in a drunken stupor. I felt ashamed of myself every single time. The next day I'd start all over again, tail between my legs, head hung low. I'd go back to AA, earnestly seeking help, desperate to "work the program."

Those periods of binge drinking were the worst for Brian. Those were the times I'm sure he knew I had a drinking problem. He saw the truth more clearly than I did. I was convinced I was hiding my problem from him. It took me years of decieving myself until I could finally speak the truth to Brian. Once I stopped lying, I no longer felt guilty or ashamed of my drinking. And I wanted to understand it.

I never felt my pattern of drinking was a "fatal disease." I kept asking questions like "Does society treat someone who is 10 pounds overweight the same as someone who is 300 pounds overweight?" The answer is no. Why then should society treat someone who consumes a couple of drinks the same as someone who is drinking a fifth of vodka or more a day, or as someone who drinks so much he or she passes out? I began doing research that supported the notion that, as with any addiction or disorder, there are different levels of drinking problems.

It seemed like such a logical argument, but one that needed more research to gain much-needed support. If I could prove my theory, that people can learn to moderate their drinking, I felt I could help a lot of people. There was a huge disconnect between moderate drinkers, social drinkers, problem drinkers, and alcoholics. I knew there was a large group who knew they had a drinking problem but didn't want to give up drinking altogether. I was one of those people. There was a tremendous need to find a program that fell somewhere between AA and no program at all.

I'd been to hundreds of AA meetings and in and out of treatment centers and rehab clinics. All of those programs were predicated on abstinence. I discovered that any time I was forced into abstinence for any extended period, I always fell off the wagon. And my backslides usually consisted of days of binge drinking. It was as if I were making up for lost time. It's no different than when dieters fall off their programs. What do they do? They binge, eating everything their body craves, which usually results in gaining back all of the weight they worked so hard to take off. Any program of abstinence has the same potential. Whenever you deprive the body of something it craves, eventually your willpower is weakened to the point of breaking a promise and fulfilling your need. Drugs, sex, food, alcohol—they're all addictions that have to be moderated or they can be deadly. I also knew that for a true chronic drinker, one slipup could be deadly. I realized it was the reason no one had developed an accepted moderation program. It was simply too risky. And yet I couldn't help thinking there had to be a way to make a moderation program work for drinkers like me.

I began to read books in the library to educate myself on alcoholism and problem drinking. One day by pure accident, I found two books that changed my life. The first was *Diseasing of America: Addiction Treatment Out of Control* by Dr. Stanton Peele, and the second was *Heavy Drinking: The Myth of Alcoholism as a Disease* by Dr. Herbert Fingarette. Both spoke about "problem drinkers" and "heavy drinkers," but they attached no label of disease to drinking. The books also gave clear guidelines on how one could reduce problem drinking. Those books and other research showed that nine out of ten problem drinkers actively and purposefully avoid traditional treatment approaches. This is because they know that most traditional programs will label them as alcoholic and will probably force attendance at 12-step and abstinence-based meetings and prescribe lifetime abstinence as the only acceptable change in drinking habits. They may also have real concerns about how their participation in these programs will affect their jobs and ability to obtain future medical and life insurance.

I wasn't the typical AA, "one drink, one drunk" drinker. I could have two drinks and stop. I could go a week or two without drinking at all. I began secretly experimenting with my drinking to test my limits and will. I abstained for a week here and there and then allowed myself to drink no more than nine glasses of wine in any given week. Sometimes I would overdrink, but usually I was well within my self-imposed limits. And if I did go over my limit, I tried to regain control so alcohol wouldn't interfere with my life. It wasn't a perfect cure, but it worked for me—for awhile anyway.

I find it interesting to know why people do the things they do.

If they got into a lot of trouble, what drove them there? How did it start? I began thinking about ways to help people like myself overcome addiction without tagging it a disease. Addicts are everywhere, but most don't know or won't admit they have an addiction. There had to be an alternative to AA for drinkers like me. If there wasn't, I was determined to create one. My gut was telling me I was onto something big.

Through my research I discovered that moderation programs did exist, but mostly in other countries, such as Sweden, Norway, Germany, Australia, New Zealand, Canada, and Great Britain. These countries all offered professional moderation-oriented programs. In the United States they have been frowned upon because of the extreme bias toward 12-step abstinence-based programs. Several books had already been written on alternative programs to the standard abstinence-based program. There are moderation programs in Great Britain where alcohol treatment centers use alcohol to teach patients how to pace themselves and drink responsibly within their own limits. They take patients to bars and help them moderate their behavior in social settings where alcohol is an everyday temptation. I thought the ideas were brilliant.

After lots of research and careful consideration, I confided to Brian that I was going to return to moderate drinking. Finally, I thought, I was going to be honest with him. I became comfortable with the role that alcohol played in my life. Once I was honest about my drinking, my urge to binge seemed to be gone. An occasional glass or two of wine became a part of my life—not the center of my life. I was able to drink moderately and maintain my daily activities and responsibilities as a wife and mother. I felt like I had found a real life again. When I chose to drink, I drank in moderation and always responsibly. From that point until March 25, 2000, I never drank and drove.

For all chronic drinkers, AA—total abstinence—is their only option if they don't want to die from drinking. I had such a hard time accepting that concept because I truly believe there is a middle ground. If my drinking had been assessed as a problem rather than a disease, and if I had been offered the option of moderation as a self-management goal when I first sought help, I believe I would never have experienced so many years of inner conflict and emotional pain.

Many people, including the court and recovery systems, have been led to believe that AA is the only "cure" for problem drinkers and alcoholics. They buy into the idea that being forced to quit will be their solution, the answer to their prayers. It's just not so. Few make it. In most meetings there are only a handful—at most half—of people who have attained real sobriety. The rest of the members are chronically in and out of the program, repeatedly getting their one-day, one-week, one-month, and one-year chips. Anytime you're forced into something against your will, it is a setup for failure. Being forced into something you don't want to do often results in the opposite outcome. To validate my perspective I attended countless AA meetings where I asked people if they had ever slipped up. Most admitted they had. But the beauty of a program like AA is that you can go back the next day with a fresh start, counting a new beginning from day one. No judgment, no guilt.

As we moved following Brian's jobs, every city brought new opportunities for growth and research. I began to look forward to new perspectives so I could continue developing what would become the foundation of Moderation Management. While we were living in Indianapolis, I saw a sign in our church that read, "Smart Recovery Meeting." In my quest for the right maintenance program for me, I wondered what this meeting was all about. A flyer for the meeting said it was a nonreligion-based program that focused more on behavior modification techniques than abstinence.

I walked into the small room where I found seven to ten people gathered. A fellow by the name of Vince Fox was running the meeting. Vince was a kind man in his 70s, who was intelligent and looked every bit the professor. He was an author who had written about alternatives to AA. I had one of his books. Although Vince didn't have a drinking problem as an adult, he had battled alcohol for a long time in his youth.

On a smoke break (people who drink like to smoke—a lot!), I began to talk to some of the people.

"Out of curiosity," I asked, "how many of you still drink?"

Almost every single person said he or she did.

"Occasionally."

"Once or twice a month."

"Only on weekends."

I couldn't understand why they admitted they were still occasional drinkers standing outside the meeting but refused to acknowledge their truth or lack of honesty about their drinking during the meeting. It made no sense to me at all. Why did these people feel the need to pretend to be abstinent when they were not? Wouldn't their treatment be more effective to admit they still drink and learn how to moderate their drinking?

I had an epiphany right there and then. What if there was a program available that helped people learn to moderate their drinking? What if I started that program? I threw the idea out there. The response was overwhelming. They all said it would be interesting and they would attend a meeting like that. We all went back inside and told Vince Fox about my idea.

Vince became a father figure to me as I grew to love and adore him. We spent days and weeks over coffee hashing out the basics of my program. Vince liked my ideas but thought I was about 10 years ahead of my time. The country simply wasn't ready for a moderation program for drinkers, he said. Even so, he encouraged me to put together a pamphlet that spelled out the general guidelines based on the literature I had read and research I had done. I reached out to several professors, asking them to help me create the program I called Moderation Management.

Moderation Management (MM) is a behavioral change program and national support group network for people concerned about their drinking and who desire to make positive lifestyle changes. MM empowers individuals to accept personal responsibility for choosing and maintaining their own path, whether that's moderation or abstinence. MM promotes early self-recognition of risky drinking behavior, when moderate drinking is a more easily achievable goal.

MM is a nine-step professionally reviewed program, which provides information about alcohol, moderate drinking guidelines and limits, self-evaluation exercises, drink-monitoring exercises, goal-setting techniques, and self-management strategies. As a major part of the program, members also use the nine steps to find balance and moderation in all areas of their lives, one small step at a time. Step Two of the program suggests that MM members abstain from alcohol for 30 days. This allows members to experience a substantial period of abstinence before going on to the moderation part of the program, and it helps them make an informed choice between moderation and abstinence. Some people find the abstinence period strengthens their commitment to change. Others find it more difficult and need to take a look at whether or not moderation is the right solution for their lifestyle. Abstinence was hard for me. I could do the mandated 30 days with no concern. I could even do a second 30 days of abstinence. But it was difficult for me to go much beyond that without drinking and feeling the urge to binge.

When I created MM, I purposely left out answering to or giving up control to a higher power. Although Brian and I shared a faith in God, we weren't terribly religious people. Off and on all my life I have had a curiosity about God. When I was a little girl, my mother took us to a Lutheran church. In high school I went through an intense period of questioning God. In college I studied philosophy of religion. As an adult, my dad shared with me a book called *The Urantia Book*. It is similar to the Bible and was first published by the Urantia Foundation in 1955. Its message is that all human beings are one family, the sons and daughters of one God, the Universal Father. The book presents a unique and compelling portrayal of the life and teachings of Jesus. Its view on science, philosophy, and religion is perhaps the clearest and most concise integration of these subjects I have read. My belief has always been that we can learn from parts of every religion, that God speaks to us in many ways. This book spoke to me.

I've always been a woman who needed to feel in control. Giving up control, especially to a higher power, was not something I had ever really done. I always believed in the American dream: Work hard, climb the ladder, make your own decisions, and you'll receive everything you want. I always let my mind rule my heart.

In my mind, God gave us a brain for a reason. To think, act, be, and do. We're supposed to use it. He commands us to love Him with all our heart, mind, and soul. Sometimes I lean a little too far toward overthinking something and not allowing circumstances merely to unfold. I spent most of my life trying to direct the outcome of things—good and bad. I couldn't embrace that anyone else had that control over our lives. So when creating the guidelines for MM, I was aware of not wanting to insert too much of my own personal belief system into the structure. I looked at the MM handbook more as a diet book than a typical step-type program. Members of MM could have their own spiritual beliefs but would not be forced to have a particular faith or a mandatory belief in God. It turned out that many people who attended MM already had strong spiritual beliefs anyway. Over time I discovered that the people who really excelled in the program were reaching out spiritually as well. That was part of their recovery.

Looking back I wish I had used some spiritual guidelines in creating the nine-step plan. God is a part of everything whether we acknowledge it or not. I have learned to take a step back and be patient because answers always come. Sometimes those answers are what I hoped for; other times, not. But have no doubt, the answers do come.

When my son, Samuel, was a little boy, I often took him and Lindsey to play in the neighborhood park. We would play with abandon, laugh, and share warm, wonderful days together. Samuel has asthma, so I monitored him to be sure he wasn't getting too worked up. One day he stood motionless several yards away from where I was playing with Lindsey. I looked over and became concerned that he might be suffering an asthma attack. He was staring up at the sky, remaining very still. I ran over to see what was wrong.

"Samuel. What are you doing? What's the matter?"

"I'm looking at God." His voice was so innocent.

I thought, "How beautiful. How simple. How pure." I was silenced by his ethereal connection.

The next morning as I was helping Samuel put on his shoes and getting him ready for preschool, he asked, "Mom, where does God live?"

For the second time in two days, I found myself facing some interesting questions. I had to answer my son, but how? For years I believed God was unknowable and unfathomable, that there was no way to describe Him. I never felt one single word could encapsulate this great force or how I felt. It was beyond words. I always felt conflicted by that inability to connect with God when I was a child. Now here was my son, so certain and secure in his own beliefs. It was innate because I hadn't passed that unshakable faith on to him as a child.

After careful thought I replied, "God lives in your heart."

Samuel seemed completely satisfied with my response. I breathed a sigh of relief. He was unnaturally calm, just as he had been the previous day. As I finished tying his shoe, he turned to me, stared for a moment, and asked, "But God is good, right?"

"Yes. God is very good."

"Well, if He lives in everybody's heart, how can people do so many bad things?"

Again I was dumbfounded. His wisdom and grace overwhelmed me. I wanted to soak in the enormous impact of his question and make sure I formulated an answer that was thoughtful and meaningful. Clearly Samuel was seeking answers that would impact his views for the rest of his life. I had to be cautious in thinking through my response.

"God lives in your heart, but He allows you the freedom to choose what direction your actions take."

With that I sent Samuel off to school. I stood in the doorway, deep in thought of the words I had just passed down to my 4-year-old son. Though I knew I had given him the "right" answer, I was keenly aware that there was absolutely no meaning behind that answer in my own heart. The more I thought about my exchange with Samuel, the more convinced I became that it was Samuel who opened my eyes and taught me something important that day—not the other way around. Perhaps I needed to examine my personal relationship with God. It was a reminder that I had left God out of my own life. This epiphany would strengthen my faith in years to come.

My basic premise in creating MM was that behaviors can be changed. I was certain of it. I had read study after study, collected enormous amounts of literature, and even conducted my own experiments, and I had figured out that there were lots of people like myself who could benefit from learning how to moderate their drinking. I didn't need a fifth of vodka every time I chose to drink a glass of wine. Over the years I discovered that controlled drinking was an issue millions of people faced every day. Like me, these people did not consider themselves alcoholics, and yet they had a problem keeping their drinking within certain limits. I was one of those people, and I felt that I had the power and the desire to change. I needed to learn the tools to affect that change to live a happier, healthier, more productive life.

I completed my MM pamphlet, which laid out the premise of the program, the nine steps, and some personal stories to illustrate why I created MM. I gave the pamphlet to Vince to read. He was impressed with my writing style and my grasp of the research and material. Unbeknownst to me, he sent my booklet to a publisher. A few weeks later I received a call from See Sharp Press, a niche publishing house in Tucson, Arizona, offering me a book deal. I never thought about becoming a professional writer. But then again, I certainly never saw myself as an advocate either. I was flattered, even though there was no money offered, and I wasn't sure the book would see the light of day. But it did.

A few months later I received a modest advance from Random House in New York. This unexpected opportunity allowed Brian to take four months off to help with my newfound career. Although he was cautious at first, Brian became active in helping me run MM. He handled the media, helped me shop for clothes for television appearances, and read what I wrote, often giving me suggestions to help make my point clear and concise. For the first time in our marriage, we began working together as a team toward a mutual goal. We connected in a way I never expected. For a while, it was bliss.

Sheryl

12 Meeting Danny

I DROPPED OUT OF HIGH SCHOOL IN 1981 BECAUSE I WAS having difficulties dealing with the pressure and abuse at home. I was 17 years old and worked as a carhop at a fast food restaurant and as a cook at another fast-food joint. I had to make money so I could continue paying my mom and dad anywhere from $200 to $400 a month in rent. Failure to do so meant my parents would kick me out of the house.

When I turned 18, I went to work as a part-time, live-in nanny for a family I had been babysitting for since I was 12. The mother, Cindy, worked as the head waitress at the Cattleman's Restaurant in Toppenish, Washington, a small town near Yakima. I grew fairly close to Cindy. I could talk to her about almost anything. She had three lovely little girls, and I spent so much time with them they became like my little sisters. One thing did bother me: Cindy and her husband were heavy drinkers. I still harbored a lot of anger toward heavy drinkers because of my dad's drunk driving crash, but alcohol never interfered with our relationship.

In late August 1982, as Labor Day weekend approached, Cindy asked me if I would like to fill in as a hostess at the restaurant. Most of her staff was planning to be away for the holiday weekend, leaving the restaurant shorthanded. I needed extra money, and it sounded like a lot of fun, so I agreed to help out.

Within minutes of arriving at the restaurant, I met one of the waiters, who I thought was cute. I stood in the kitchen talking with him. In the background I caught sight of a young-looking boy walking through the kitchen, darting here and there, singing; he was definitely trying to attract my attention. He looked like he was about 12 years old, too young to be a cook, so I assumed he was a busboy. Out of nowhere this kid whipped out a pocket camera and snapped a photo of me. I was startled by the flash and confused as to why this geeky boy was taking my picture. I turned to the cute waiter and asked him to take away the camera. But the boy refused to give it up. "I want to have a picture of the woman I am meant to love," he said. That boy turned out to be my future husband, Danny.

For a long time after, the family I worked for kept pushing me to go out with "Danny from the restaurant." I wasn't especially attracted to him at first, but the family kept encouraging me to give him a chance. I learned that despite his young-looking face, Danny was two years older than me. The family told me what a nice guy he was and that I ought to go on a date. At the time I was dating my high school sweetheart. Even though our relationship was a bit tumultuous, I thought he was "the one." That is until the day I received a letter from him telling me he was cheating on me. Then he said, "Ha. Ha. Just wanted to see what you would say." It was such high school drama! Still, I was numb from his admission. I didn't know what to do. I loved my boyfriend, but I wasn't going to tolerate his bull anymore. So I did what any girl would do. I decided to move on. I marched down to the Cattleman's Restaurant, threw open the kitchen door, and asked Danny what time he got off work.

"Ten," he said.

"Well, good, because you're going out with me." I gave him a big kiss on the lips, turned, and walked away.

Danny was raised in the eastern Cascade Mountains in Prosser, Washington, the youngest of 13 kids. He grew up pretty poor. His biological father died from a muscular disease when Danny was only 5 years old. His stepfather was a wonderful man but could only provide minimally for such a large family. It was a close-knit family, though, that nurtured and strengthened one another. The large clan kept an eye out and always made sure everyone was safe. They described Danny as "their special boy." He was always laughing and singing, having a good time wherever he went. He was quiet yet strong. He was handsome but also a little nerdy looking, with no clue about how to dress.

As the youngest child, Danny wore clothes that were mostly hand-me-downs that were pretty worn and tattered by the time they got to him. On our first date Danny picked me up wearing a shirt that was two sizes too big, with the shoulders reaching his midarm. He folded the sleeves up several times until the folds crept above his elbows. He wore baggy worn-out corduroy gray slacks that were too loose to show off his cute behind. Finally he had on platform shoes straight out of *Saturday Night Fever.* I took one look at him and just about died. He was not my type of guy, that's for sure. Lucky for him, he was charming and funny.

Danny took me to the horse races on our first date. I had never been to Yakima Meadows race track. Gambling was frowned upon in my home and that was the last place I would have expected to go on a date. Danny pored over the racing form, studying statistics and wagering the favorites. He lost every race. As for me? I looked at the names of the horses and the colors of the jockeys' silks, and sure enough, my horses kept coming in. So Danny started betting on my guesses and we ended our day up $400. We had a blast. It was definitely the start of something special.

We celebrated our good fortune by going out to dinner at a fancy restaurant. Danny wined and dined me, making me feel like a princess. When he came to pick me up for our second date, he was a changed man. He came roaring up our driveway on his motorcycle. I opened the door and this cute guy with curly blond hair was standing there, wearing a white turtleneck, black leather jacket, and nice-fitting jeans. He handed me a little houseplant because I had told him how much I love plants and flowers.

Danny took me to the Yakima County Fair that day, not the outing I would have picked, but I'm so glad we went. We walked around until we stumbled onto a photo shop. We put on period costumes and had our picture taken. Later that night, one of Danny's twin sisters saw the picture and commented that it looked like an old wedding photo.

"You're kind of jumping the gun here, aren't you?" one said.

We both just smiled.

I didn't set out to fall in love again, but Danny and I were moving in that direction. He was only my second boyfriend. My parents liked him and approved of him. Despite the harshness of my family life, their approval mattered so much to me. I finally had met a young man they liked, and for a short time that made me feel happy. In the long run, Danny turned out to be more like my mom and dad, becoming abusive, controlling, and belittling. But in the beginning I thought I had met my prince.

Technically, Danny never asked me to marry him. We talked about our future and mutually decided a life together as husband and wife was what we both wanted. We shared a common bond in that we both sought a life partner who knew God. Danny bought me a beautiful diamond cross necklace I wore every day as a symbol of our love. We picked a date and began to plan our wedding. After many conversations about the escalating costs, we decided having a large wedding was too much of a financial burden for us. So we went to the justice of the peace and got married in May 1983, a year ahead of our original planned date. It was a small civil ceremony with just 10 close family members in attendance. The ceremony took place in the judge's chambers in the Prosser courthouse. There was no reception. Both Danny and I went to work after the ceremony. Shortly after we said our "I dos," my father gave Danny some marital advice: "Take her home and beat her. She deserves it."

That was how my dad saw me.

We moved into a small trailer in Toppenish, where Danny

continued to work as a cook. Cooking was Danny's passion. He loved being in the kitchen. His opportunities were limited, however, unless he became a chef. To do so he would have to go to culinary school, something we could not afford. So he continued working at several of the best restaurants in the region and studying cooking on the side whenever he had time, which wasn't very often because his hours were long and relentless. He left for work early in the morning, hours before the first customer arrived, and continued to work well past when the last dessert was served, plate cleared, and candles snuffed out.

Every restaurant in the area offered Danny work. He was a great cook and a good man to have in the high-pressure situations of a commercial kitchen. But if he was ever going to grow beyond his chicken, steak, and occasional seafood selections, we would have to move. We had neither the money nor the connections, however, to take the leap on our own.

We talked about options and prayed together for many hours about the situation. It became clear to us that the military was our best solution. I had always shied away from marrying a military man, given my history. But listening to Danny talk about his dreams, we decided the Army would be a good place for him to sharpen his culinary skills. He could put in his mandatory three years, earn the benefits of the GI Bill, and then go on to culinary college or whatever else he decided to do.

Danny did his basic training at Fort Dix, New Jersey, and Advanced Individual Training (AIT) at Fort Belfore, Virginia. To our astonishment, Danny loved the Army. Even though he was sent to train as a generator mechanic instead of as a cook, he remained not just happy but fulfilled. And for the first time in my life, I found myself thousands of miles away from my family, free of their judgments and abuse. Those first few years of marriage were heaven. Danny and the Army saved me from my abusive childhood and gave me more strength, peace, and security than I had ever known. We made new friends, became active in our church, and grew both as people and as a couple. We also became pregnant with our first child. It was a wonderful time for us.

When Danny's training was done, we were stationed in Fort Stewart, Georgia. We lived there for only a year, but that is where I gave birth to Zackery on December 23, 1985. I was 21 years old when I gave birth to Zack. I was healthy, weighing about 103 before I became pregnant. I gained a lot of weight during the pregnancy and battled toxemia, high blood pressure, and diabetes from the pregnancy. Since I was just one of many military wives attended by the doctor, my care was fairly minimal, with little personal attention. Sometimes 30 or 40 of us could see the doctor on a single day. I felt like we were cattle being herded through the examination room.

I became sick and almost miscarried during the first trimester. The doctors were concerned that I might have been carrying twins at one time and had lost one baby early in the pregnancy. But Zack was still alive. I was put on immediate bed rest for the duration of my pregnancy. By the time I gave birth, I had gained more than 80 pounds. The delivering physician refused to believe I barely weighed a hundred pounds before getting pregnant. I was in labor for nearly 24 hours before I went to the hospital. I was convinced my contractions were false labor. What did I know? All I had heard was that your contractions were supposed to become regularly rhythmic, and my contractions did not do that.

The delivering doctor didn't want to do a cesarean, so both Zack and I were forced to suffer through a terribly painful and dangerous delivery. The doctors had to use vacuum extractors and forceps to pull the baby out. His skull was so mangled from the pressure, it looked like he had a cone head. He had a blue bruise from the forceps, like a birthmark, on his forehead for years. It eventually faded.

After I gave birth I continued bleeding profusely. I was in a fight for my life. Had it not been for one particular doctor who happened to walk by my room, I might have died. He overrode the decision made by the attending physician and ordered blood tests and a transfusion. I was certain I was dying and said goodbye to Danny, scared that I might not be able to say it if I waited any longer. Then I slipped out of consciousness. I don't know how long I was out or what happened.

The doctors revived me.

"Sheryl. Wake up, Sheryl. Can you hear me? Do you know where you are?"

I answered "Yes."

The doctors never asked me if I knew I was in a hospital. They accepted my answer as an affirmation that I was aware of where I was. But for all they knew, I could have thought I was on a beach in Florida or safely in my own bed at home.

I never fully recovered from that trauma. To this day I fight fatigue all the time as a result.

Zack and I came home from the hospital the day after Christmas, but he woke up the next day yellow with jaundice. I was still so sick when we took him to the pediatric hospital, the nurses checked me back in too. They wanted to make sure I was keeping fluids in me and that I rested until I was completely out of danger. I should not have been released in the first place, but the military hospital had delivered nearly 300 babies that December and expected more, and they needed my bed.

Life returned to normal. Danny and I had our beautiful son, and we were a family. Not long after Zack was born, Danny received orders that he was to be deployed to a U.S. Army base in Aschaffenburg, Germany. I couldn't have been more thrilled. To me Germany was home, that's where I'd spent most of my childhood. Sadly, I was forced to remain stateside with our now 6-month-old baby when Danny shipped out because I was still too weak from giving birth to travel.

I joined Danny a few months later in October 1986. He was supposed to have two weeks' leave to help us settle. Instead, a few hours after I arrived, Danny was placed on alert, which meant he had no idea where he was going or for how long, but he was definitely leaving his wife and baby all alone. There are only two reasons for an alert: either NATO had called for top secret training or Danny was going to war.

Danny was sworn to secrecy. He could tell no one where he was headed, not his family, friends, fellow soldiers, or his church. All I could do was pray to God that everything would be all right, Danny would come back safe, and Zack would stay healthy.

But it was not meant to be. Zack became sick. More than likely, he picked up a bug on the flight over to Germany, because I also got sick after the trip. Fortunately Danny had found an apartment for us right across the street from the base. The location made it easy for me to take Zack to the doctor.

Our lovely little apartment was on the third floor of a three-story townhouse in the beautiful picturesque German village of Aschaffenburg. But it became a prison of sorts. After Danny left we were on our own. I had no idea where he was, how long he'd be gone, or if he would even come back. Most of Danny's fellow soldiers were not married, so I had no camaraderie among the women on base. Every time I walked out the door, I was a stranger, lost in this strange place. Though I had lived in Germany as a child, my language skills were limited. I could barely tell a taxi driver where I wanted to go. I had virtually no money, which made things even tougher because I couldn't comfort myself by buying extra things like toys for the baby or something pretty to wear for myself. I felt helpless. I felt alone. I felt scared and worried about the future for my baby and myself.

Audrey

13 MM Meetings

I FINISHED WRITING *MODERATE DRINKING* IN 1993 WITH the hope that it would become the official MM handbook. I created several versions of the pamphlet and used them as the unofficial handbook during the first few meetings of MM. They looked more like pamphlets than a manuscript, but I spent hours at Kinko's editing and printing each new edition. It was time to test my theory.

Brian and I were now living in Ann Arbor, Michigan. I placed an ad in the local paper that read, "If you think you have a drinking problem and you'd like support to cut back or quit drinking, meet at the Unitarian Church Monday at 7:00."

I was unsure if anyone would show up, but I had to take the risk. I instinctively knew I wasn't alone in my quest to learn moderation. But AA was such a well-respected and established entity. Would people be open-minded enough to see the potential of a moderation program such as MM? My thoughts and ideas were new to most drinkers. Everything they had heard pointed in the direction of the fundamentals of AA, not my ideas for MM.

Only a few people trickled in that first meeting. I was uncomfortable and worried that maybe I had made a horrible mistake. I wanted more people to know that there were alternatives to AA. I hoped that beginning-stage problem drinkers would come to learn more information, which I felt was being kept from them by other groups. In my mind, MM would help people before they developed a problem with alcohol. I knew from personal experience that a lot of people can be intimidated by going to AA, their doctor, or even other support groups because that act alone indicates they believe they have a problem. Nobody knew anything about my program or the basic premise behind it, so there should have been no stigma. I wasn't sure how many high-functioning problem drinkers actually read the paper, let alone the small advertisement for our first meeting. Unlike AA, where referrals are the primary source of newcomers to the program, there was no one referring people to MM—not yet anyway.

Critics initially viewed MM as a program to teach alcoholics how to moderate. They thought I wanted to give alcoholics an escape route from abstinence. That was not the foundation of MM. I had to take a deep breath and hold on to my belief that the people who came to the first meeting were just like me. I desperately wanted them to relate to my stories and journey to moderation. One woman said she had come because she had just given birth to twins. For the first time in her life, she had become a nip-here-nip-there drinker. It had become a coping mechanism for the struggles she was having with motherhood and juggling all of the chaos. She easily admitted her drinking was affecting many facets of her life. I completely embraced her story. I had been there too.

As the first 30 days passed, MM members reported on the progress of their abstinence—their struggles but also their newfound confidence to make it through the first 30-day period. When they began learning to drink within their limits, people confided that some weeks were easier than others. They admitted to blowing their limits or reducing their usual intake. During our meetings there was an openness and trust that grew between our members, which reminded me of AA. This fact alone offered great hope that MM could become a viable program.

Occasionally people from AA sat in on meetings. A lot of them were old-timers who wanted to find out what our program was all about. I could always tell newcomers to AA the minute they walked through the door. Their body language was defensive, and they winced at the notion that MM was a program that gave alcoholics permission to drink. But, if they listened closely, inevitably they understood that our meetings were not intended to be AA meetings. Our members were not chronic drinkers. Alcoholics were not our target market. Our meetings were trying to help the problem drinker figure out if he or she could drink. Almost always the AA members who attended our meetings left with a completely different impression than they had come with to our meetings. If an AA newcomer challenged our ideas, I often referred to a passage found in the *Big Book* (the AA bible) that refers to moderation:

"Then, we have a certain type of hard drinker. He may have the habit badly enough to gradually impair him physically and mentally. It may cause him to die a few years before his time. If a sufficiently strong reason, ill health, falling in love, change of environment or the warning of a doctor becomes operative, this man can also stop or moderate."

I pointed to the fact that the word "moderate" is actually used in the *Big Book* of AA.

AA also admits there is a difference between a problem drinker and a real alcoholic. The *Big Book* says, "Although he may find it difficult, troublesome and may even need medical attention. But what about the real alcoholic?"

My interpretation of that thought is someone can be completely functioning, be in a relationship, have a good job, have no health problems, and can stop or moderate his or her drinking if sufficiently motivated. The whole idea of MM was to give this kind of problem drinker a place to go to find out if moderation, or at least reduced drinking, was an option. The hope was that the problem drinker would discover his or her path before losing everything important in their lives.

Gradually MM meetings began to grow in attendance and in the number of locations where meetings were held. I posted the MM manual on the Internet, making it available to those people who wanted to research what MM was all about. They could print the manual and start their own groups, which started happening all over the country. Once groups began in other states, the people running those sessions could take over the responsibilities of answering questions and giving information that had been solely my own. I was elated, but it was a constant struggle. My perseverance and hard work were beginning to pay off, but starting and running MM was a financial strain on my family. I wasn't being paid for my time or services, and I had no idea how to raise money to help pay for the overhead. Receiving thousands of letters meant answering thousands of letters. The postage alone was overwhelming, let alone the time commitment involved in answering them. But I felt good knowing I was helping others. The joy of knowing other people were making positive life changes as a result of something I did was unlike anything I had ever known. I felt like a real person with a genuine purpose. My dark, lonely years of living a lie finally had meaning.

Unlike AA, the turnover rate in MM meetings was pretty significant because the program is designed to help people figure out ways to manage or quit drinking and then move on with their lives. Some MM members chose to leave for AA. Others felt they had control over their drinking and were no longer in need of our maintenance and support. About this time I showed my final manuscript to Dr. Ernest Kurtz, a recognized authority on abstinence as well as on the history and development of AA. I met Dr. Kurtz after moving to Ann Arbor. I was honored to have him review my manuscript.

His response was astounding: "Audrey, very soon your program will refer more people to AA than any other single program or issue in the entire world."

His words were so meaningful because they showed that MM could help people find their way through their addiction, whether that meant abstinence or moderation. My hope was that MM would help them conquer their addiction before they lost everything.

The Detroit News picked up on MM, running a fairly long article detailing the work I was doing. The Associated Press syndicated the article and within a few weeks, little Audrey Kishline and Moderation Management were causing quite a stir in the national news. *The New York Times,* the *Los Angeles Times,* and many papers from coast to coast ran the story. All of the major talk shows began to call too. *Leeza, Dateline, 48 Hours,* even *Oprah!* AA came out vehemently against MM. They utterly disagreed with the program. MM was a topic during AA meetings. I received requests for interviews from all over the world. Phone calls and letters began to pour in by the bucketful from people wanting to know more about the program and how to find a copy of my still unreleased book.

I was overwhelmed by the response. Brian was very happy. Not only was I helping others, I was helping myself and in return our relationship, which had suffered terribly from my drinking. I was being honest with Brian about my drinking. It was under control. I was active, involved, and I was happy.

Moderation Management was founded as a nonprofit organization. Meetings were free. I was funding the organization out of my own pocket and through the nominal donations members made from time to time. I didn't have the proper funding or staff to support the infrastructure of the organization I was building faster than expected. Within 12 weeks of the first *The Detroit News* article, MM programs were up and running in 28 states and Canada. As the program grew, so did the controversy. I was shocked my program was causing so much turmoil, but Vince Fox had warned me my ideas were ahead of their time. He had expressed his concern that society wasn't ready to hear about a program like MM, and he was right. It seemed like everyone wanted the chance to poke holes in my ideas on moderation—it made for some good television.

My first national television appearance was in March 1995 when I appeared on *Leeza.* From the moment my plane landed in Los Angeles, I was thrown into Hollywood. I had a limousine, an agent, a limousine, an agent, a cell phone, the hustle, the hair and makeup, the frantic electric air of totally focused energy before the taping, and it was all directed at me. I was not used to this kind of attention, and I hated how it felt. The Hollywood hustle and flow was way out of my league. I was a middle-class suburban housewife and mother who drank a little more than I should. Surely Hollywood had seen worse. What was the draw? Why was there so much attention on my obscure ideas about alcohol moderation?

I was about to find out. Right between the eyes. Kapow!

What I didn't know was the producers of *Leeza* had decided to create a confrontational atmosphere designed to debunk my philosophy and ideas. They brought together for the show a group of doctors and scientists who were strongly opposed to what they thought I was representing.

Welcome to Hollywood!

I quickly found out that the other guests scheduled to be on the show that day, the producers, and even Leeza Gibbons hadn't bothered to read my book. They had based their entire hour of programming on hype and hearsay. Worse yet, the producers filled the audience with regional AA groups and people from neighboring treatment centers they bused in from all over Southern California. I had no idea I was about to walk into the lion's den. My first clue was when the producer came into the makeup room, pointed his finger like a gun at me, and said, "OK, Audrey. Give us a good show!"

I wasn't there to entertain. I had agreed to appear on the show to educate. This was serious business to me. I was nervous, very nervous. I was brought out onto the stage and caught a glimpse of the show title as it zipped across the studio monitor: "New Program to Teach Alcoholics How to Drink Again."

There I sat—all alone on this huge stage, staring at the studio audience who were now looking at me as if I was about to be fresh kill. Beads of sweat began building on my forehead.

The cameras were all focused on me. I froze for a second and then realized I had to correct the notion that MM was a program aimed at people in recovery. It most certainly was not. I explained to Leeza and the audience that MM was intended to help people who thought they might have a drinking problem, who were afraid they could be in trouble. I went on to make my point by emphasizing that acknowledged alcoholics were not welcome at MM meetings.

The more I spoke, the more feverishly I defended MM. My fear melted under the hot studio lights. I was never clearer about my mission or purpose. In the process I threw the entire show off balance. They hadn't expected me to be so fervent. Leeza was at a loss. Her producers hadn't prepared her for the truth or premise behind MM. They were failing in their aim to demolish me on camera—miserably.

Taping was abruptly stopped. The producer was livid, insisting the show start again from the top. He threatened to cancel the taping altogether if I didn't agree to begin again. I glanced toward Brian, who was sitting in the front row, and asked, "What do you think I should do?" This was a big moment in our lives. The very future of MM depended on this decision. I needed to know that my husband stood beside me to either move forward or walk away. Brian was clearly as stressed as I was, but I could see his eyes. I looked deep into his knowing eyes and heard him say, "Let them do it."

After a short break we began again. But this time the doctors who had been brought on to refute me and trash my program were saying that it was a good idea whose time had come. Some drinkers, if their problem is caught early enough, can indeed learn to moderate. The only time the essence of the original show seeped through was during the audience question segment. Their questions came out sounding as if they were rigged—which they were.

For example: "I lost everything to drugs and alcohol. Do you think I should start drinking again?"

Clearly, that was not my opinion. The question was written on a

5×7 card word for word. The questions were blatantly manipulated to punch tiny holes in my platform, but it didn't work. When the taping was over, I had never felt more secure that I was on the right path.

Leeza served to propel me even further into the spotlight. The experts brought on to defeat me ended up defending MM. My moderation program was taking on a new life, one that began to grow into a phenomenon, including coverage in *Newsweek* (March 27, 1995).

By the time I appeared on *Oprah* nine months later, I was much more comfortable in front of the cameras and live audiences. Even so, Brian always comforted me when I became panic-ridden or irritable just before a taping. Much of that behavior was due to not eating very much for days before I did a show because my nerves overrode my appetite.

The news magazine show *48 Hours* was doing a feature story on me around the same time I was asked to appear on *Oprah*. They had asked to follow me around, including taping me throughout the *Oprah* appearance. Ignorant to exclusivity in television news, I foolishly and innocently agreed. Oprah's producers went crazy when they found out. How could I agree to such a thing? This was their show. I was such a newcomer to the high-pressure world of national television, I had no idea I was breaking a cardinal rule. I felt horrible. Oprah, with her popularity and power, was the last person I wanted to upset. I knew what it meant to anger her staff.

Once again Brian came to the rescue, mediating both sides to make sure everyone was satisfied with the compromise. My respect and affection for him deepened because of his loving support of my work.

Oprah and her team did a tremendous job preparing for our taping. They thoroughly researched MM, identifying local MM groups and interviewing several participants. They even taped Oprah entering a local bar and asking the patrons about their drinking habits. She asked how often they drank and how much, whether they ever hid their drinking, and so on.

During the taping Oprah was careful to describe MM as a program for people who might have a drinking problem. Hands down, she was by far the most professional in both her attitude and depth of coverage.

There's a saying in AA circles: "Secrets are what kill you." After nine months of exposing my soul in the national media, from *Leeza* to *Oprah* and many other shows in between, I finally felt free. The entire country had heard my story—the good, the bad, and the ugly. For the first time in years, I had nothing to hide. I was telling the world, "This is who I am." And the world was embracing me like a mother holding her child. I felt safe, protected, and secure.

Brian saw me blossom during those months. He helped me prepare for appearances by taking long walks with me while rehearsing answers and dialogue. He came to all of the television interviews. It was very comforting to me to see him sitting in the audience. Knowing he was there gave me enough courage to face any tough question and to debate the validity of what I believed in so very much.

Brian became more active in MM. He was on the board of directors, helping make decisions and guiding the organization in every way he could. Brian helped set up MM chat rooms on the Internet. Over time more people researched MM through the Internet than via live meetings. Everything in my life was on track. My marriage, my family, my career, my self-esteem, and my drinking. I was writing, talking to reporters, spreading my message, researching, helping others, and building much needed self-confidence. For a period of two years, from incarnation to full swing, I was the most productive and functional I had ever been.

14 Facing Demons

AFTER ZACK'S BIRTH I MADE A DECISION TO START down a path of self-discovery and realization so I could invite some true happiness into my life. As a mother and wife, I knew I had some issues from my past that needed to heal before I could be the best version of myself for my family. OK, I'll admit, I got a lot of my self-realization from watching *Oprah*. But honestly, she is so smart, and I believe she really wants to help women heal their wounds. She frequently talks about her own abuse as a child and how she overcame the emotional toll it took on her life.

Zack was just 10 months old when he and I joined Danny in Germany. When Danny was away I began to spend a lot of time at the soldiers' center on the base, where the chaplain's office was located. Once Danny returned I continued to go there often. Sometimes Zack and I waited for Danny to get off work. Other times I went there wanting to talk to the chaplain about whatever was on my mind. Danny and I were beginning to become involved in the church on the base. We talked about wanting God to be a bigger presence in our lives and striving to live true Christian lives. Chaplain Dougherty helped us work toward that goal both as a couple and as individuals. Every day was an opportunity to know God better.

While Danny had long had strong faith, I had some catching up to do. As a child I ran away from God. Our family preacher always said things like "God is your father," which scared me. Throughout my childhood, my only image of men was that they were mean, abusive, and hateful, so I was petrified at the thought that God was my father. The chaplain was like the type of dad I saw in the movies. He was warm, kind, caring, and thoughtful, unlike most of the men I grew up around. He never saw me as rotten or bad and always gave me a sense of comfort that I could talk to him about anything without worrying about being judged. When we spoke it was as if I were talking with an old friend.

After many hours of talking to Chaplain Dougherty about my abusive childhood experiences, he explained that knowing God would help me heal from all of my unresolved turmoil. He could see I was in terrible emotional pain and in dire need of God's love. He convinced me that God would protect me and love me no matter what or who I was. God loved me even if my mother and father called me the vilest names imaginable and treated me with hatred and contempt. I had never known that kind of acceptance or unconditional love. I lived and breathed to have that kind of warm embrace. I instinctively knew how to give that kind of love, but until the chaplain told me otherwise, I never believed I was worthy to receive it.

I spoke to Danny about my desire to move closer to God. I explained that I thought God would help us have a better relationship and stronger marriage, plus improve our parenting and teach us how to communicate on a higher level. Danny had talked about the importance of God in his life from the beginning of our relationship, even before we married, so he didn't need convincing. Although we had gone to church with my mother and siblings when we were dating, it wasn't until we joined a Bible study group with my cousin and his wife back in Washington that we had truly embraced what God could bring into our lives.

Danny and I began living a more committed Christian life, trying each day to live by the Word of God. We committed to a life of no drinking (which we never did anyway), no cursing (which was a little more of a challenge), and regularly attending Bible study and church. Danny joined the church choir, and we began regularly attending

Sunday school and helping in the community by volunteering our time to worthy causes. We dedicated ourselves to learning more about God and His will. The more I investigated faith, the clearer it became that there is great power in prayer. As I looked back on my life, I identified many instances when God brought me through dangers and difficulties because of my prayers.

Danny was a man of great faith, but he wasn't someone who always believed in prayer. I remembered one night, not long after we had married and were still living in Washington, Danny and I were out for a drive along an old highway from Toppenish to Mabton. There's nothing but open road and vast lands between those two points. Danny had forgotten to fill the car up with gas before we left, and the needle was teetering just below "E" on the fuel gauge. I kept telling Danny, "Let's just pray. We'll make it to a gas station. I know we will." Danny laughed at the thought that prayer would deliver us 30 miles to the next gas station. But it did.

"See what prayer can do?" I boasted to Danny as he filled up the tank.

Even so, Danny never seemed to embrace the power of prayer. He saw the world in black and white, and prayer was too gray for him. Me? I grew up believing that anything was possible. In spite of all the reasons the world offered me to hate, I made it a priority to just love. The chaplain saw the love in my heart, but he also understood I was still wounded from my past. He encouraged me to face down my demons as a way to emotionally free myself from the chokehold of my past. He suggested I visit the apartment we lived in as a child and purge all of the negative feelings attached to that time in my life. They were suffocating and depriving me of living a happy life.

Danny and I went to the apartment in Frankfurt. I remembered exactly where it was. I couldn't give you directions there, but my heart led me to the front door. I knocked on the door and asked if I could come in. I explained the reason I was there—that I had grown up in that apartment and I needed closure on some bad things that had happened in that home. The tenants graciously let me in. I walked around, slowly taking in the importance of being there. I went into my old bedroom, stood quiet, and finally faced down my demons. So many memories flooded my mind. Bad memories.

All of the abuse, the hitting, the screaming, the lies, the betrayal. And there was more. There was sexual abuse. Every moment of all of those years, moments I'd closed off in my mind for years, was in front of me. It wasn't easy, but I forgave myself for what had happened to me. After all, I was just a child; it wasn't my fault. There had been no one to protect me or keep me safe. My heart guided my choice to try to forgive the man, my dad's best friend, who caused me so much pain. To forgive my mother for her actions. To forgive my father for ignoring the obvious and adding to my pain. But most of all, for my own well-being, I no longer wanted to carry the burden of someone else's—of his—wrongdoings. It was a cleansing that could only have taken place in the same house where all of this damage was done.

It was a moment of clarity and release. The heaviness that weighed on my heart for years was gone. I felt free. I felt vindicated. I was finally able to let go of all that had been holding me down for so many years. My nightmares were over and I began to heal. I could feel my heart open as the anger and resentment faded away. I had told Danny about the abuse before, but like my parents he never believed me. Not until that moment. As a couple we were never closer than we were that day.

Things were better than ever after that experience. We were growing spiritually and emotionally, supporting one another in healthy ways at home and in our outside interests. I joyfully watched Danny turn his love of cooking into a form of service and outreach. Our church and Bible study group hosted a meal every weekend for any soldier who wished to come. The chaplain of our base called these outreach evenings Sunday Night Live. Danny and I were determined to give something back to our military community, even if it was only one hot meal a week. It meant something to all of us.

Life in the Army is hard, full of temptations. Too many soldiers get sucked into a hard-partying lifestyle, especially the soldiers who aren't married. Most soldiers have never been away from home before joining the Army. Suddenly they find themselves thrust into a life where survival means fitting in and being part of a unit. They are taught to follow orders and hold hard to them. Come what may, their lives depend on being a member of their group. For far too many of these young people, belonging means living by a code of "work hard, play harder."

Our church's Sunday outreach dinners served a far greater purpose than giving soldiers a place to pass another lonely night. Far from home and tired from too much partying, many soldiers hungered for something more. Many were lost souls searching for something they couldn't recognize. I understood that feeling because it had taken me years to trust that God will always be there. These soldiers were not the type to turn to God or the church for warmth or support. These were soldiers who wanted to watch a football game and eat some home cooking with their friends. They longed for a sense of "home" in their faraway military world. They gravitated toward what was different, even if they couldn't put what they were searching for into words.

Danny's dinners helped bridge that gap. Children were always welcome. They sang and played as the adults talked and laughed. Couples held hands. Friends gathered in a place where the focus was on togetherness. There was no alcohol or any drugs allowed— no exceptions.

Danny always served as head chef for these functions, which was no easy task. He never knew how many people would show up from week to week. It ranged anywhere from six to 60. The Army hall we were assigned had a nice kitchen, but sometimes it wasn't sufficient for our needs. One Thanksgiving we served more than 300 guests. It was awesome. We were all people away from home who got together to celebrate Thanksgiving as one big family. Danny cooked more than 20 turkeys in kitchens all around the base to accommodate the unexpected but welcome crowd. I followed right behind him, making sure every kitchen he cooked in was spotless after we left.

The Army taught Danny and me to be a family. We found ways to serve the community, to reach beyond our own lives and share the lessons of our faith with others. We did not find perfection; that is a never-ending quest. Nothing in life had ever led us to expect an easy road. We remained humble about our failings, of which we had many. But our simple faith continued to grow and emerge as a strong and powerful force in our lives. We spent so much quality time together with close friends we made on the base and through our church and Bible groups. Although they weren't family by blood, our friends were nonetheless our family. I felt I was in a place I truly belonged.

15 Falling Apart

ONE OF THE MOST IMPORTANT MESSAGES I WANTED TO convey in MM was that drinking should never endanger someone else. Unfortunately I didn't stress that in my first book. Drinkers (and addicts in general) usually tend to be selfish people who don't give much thought to the impact their behavior may be having on their family, friends, and even strangers. MM was created to be a program of awareness. It was meant to help people take a moral and physical inventory of the impact that consuming alcohol was having on their everyday lives.

A couple years after starting MM, I began to drink more heavily than the guidelines set forth in the program. I still denied I was a genuine alcoholic, though it was evident that my drinking was beginning to cause problems in my life. I did see myself as a problem drinker, one who binged from time to time, just like my dad did when I was growing up. There were plenty of times my drinking was not "moderate" when I was running MM. To be clear, the crash that killed Danny and LaShell could have happened at any one of a number of periods in my life because I was irresponsible and stupidly drank and drove many times over the years. It was not MM that caused my crash. It was my foolish choice to drink excessively and drive. The program is clear: The first of the MM Limits reads, "Never drive while under the influence of alcohol" (*Moderate Drinking,* page 162). I had stated the obvious but chose to remain oblivious.

I was sliding from being a problem drinker to a heavy drinker whose life was spinning out of control. I never knew where or when I crossed that line. It just happened.

Two years after starting MM, I realized something wasn't right with my own moderation management. I began to feel anxious all the time. I was unhappy, depressed, and numb partially because I was in a marriage that was no longer working. I worried about the smallest things, such as whether I washed my hands before cooking dinner, and about much bigger issues, such as whether or not Brian would lose his job or whether that gnawing pain in my stomach might be stomach cancer. My worry spun and spun until my thoughts were out of control. I was diagnosed with anxiety disorder, but I refused to accept the analysis and stopped taking my medication within months of starting MM.

There doesn't have to be a specific cause to bring on panic or anxiety for someone with anxiety disorder. Alcohol helped relieve my anxiety, but eventually I had to drink more and more to achieve the same result. Whenever I stopped drinking, my anxiety resurfaced. Brian knew I was drinking over my limits, but he had no clue how often. I mostly kept my drinking a secret from him, primarily choosing to binge while he was out of town on business. While MM initially had a positive impact on my marriage, it ultimately led to the demise of our relationship.

Being in the media spotlight put enormous stress on me. I was never comfortable doing interviews. I worried I might say the wrong thing, and if I did, what would the fallout be? After several years I also began losing my passion for MM. I needed to move on with something else, but I didn't know which direction to go. I was stumbling around looking for another purpose. I wrote a screenplay called *Age Rage* about women struggling with getting older. I wrote another screenplay about a young girl trying to figure out who she really was. I tried to put my focus on something creative, but nothing seemed to guide me toward a happier place.

I continued running MM and said nothing of my struggles. I

knew in my heart I could never stop drinking. I was afraid to admit my failure to moderate to anyone, especially anyone in MM.

As hard as I tried to make things work, my home life was a big part of my problem. I was unhappy and dissatisfied in my relationship, yet I was afraid to leave Brian. Sometimes couples just grow apart. Brian's goals were different from mine, and we had different ways of communicating. When Brian became angry, his voice got louder, which devastated me. I grew up in a family where no one yelled—ever. I felt attacked when Brian raised his voice, but I didn't have enough strength or self-esteem to tell him how I felt, so I just said nothing. The only thing we had left to talk about was the kids. We lost our friendship, not our love. I wanted the freedom to be and do whatever I wanted. Even so, I didn't know if I had the strength or courage to make it on my own. My history had always been jumping from one relationship to the next. I had never been single as an adult. Also I was afraid to leave because Brian and I had two children to think about. I didn't want to make a decision that would harm them. I felt trapped where I was—a prisoner in my own life.

I was failing at my own program. Once again I was living a lie. As MM group members confessed their failures, I pretended to prevail. I gave others hope when I knew I couldn't manage my own addiction. I was burned out from my overloaded schedule and the constant juggling to keep MM financially afloat. There was no need for me to continue creating anything because MM was now a self-sufficient organization. Writing had become a passion, yet I had no outlet for my words, thoughts, ideas, and stories. I toyed with writing fiction and screenplays. My sister Nicole is a successful novelist and film producer. We collaborated on a few projects, but nothing came from it.

All the major truths in life involve a paradox—even if you can't see it at the time. I didn't feel I was living an authentic life, true to my own self. But I didn't know how to change. I knew I had flaws. God gave me an Achilles heel—alcohol. I have to believe that God has His reasons, wanting us to have certain flaws that we have to deal with so we can help other people along the way.

Someone once asked me what I thought my life would be like if alcohol wasn't a daily struggle. I gave it some thought. After careful consideration I realized I have never considered the possibility.

This is my journey, the path I have chosen. I am a drinker. God gives each of us free will. We make choices in life, then live with the consequences. I think other people can see our flaws long before we do. It's like that old saying, "You can spot a flea on someone else's shoulder and miss the elephant on your own." That was me. I had no clue how far I had fallen.

I had written a book on moderation and balance, and now I found myself the least moderate and balanced woman on earth. I once heard a saying that "life is to be lived with moderation in all things, including moderation." I was crashing, but no one knew. Not even me.

Years ago, in the very first treatment center I checked into, hospital staff members told me I had a physical disease that I had no control over, a condition that was inevitably progressive. I denied it, but looking back, they were right. Further, they told me I was an alcoholic, that AA was my only cure. Now, in possibly the most defenseless and dependent stage of my life, I began to fulfill some of the prophecies set forth during that first treatment. I became a binge drinker, suddenly obsessed with either drinking too much or not at all. I felt disgraced and demoralized, forever branded with my identity as an alcoholic, amplified by my new identity as the founder of an alcohol management program. I ended up accepting that I was indeed powerless over my condition, and my self-esteem and confidence gradually disappeared as I slowly and methodically lost myself nightly in every bottle.

I had lived a double life so many times, for so long, I didn't know how to be one unified version of myself. My dual identity took so much energy that I had nothing left to give to Brian, my kids, MM, anything. My dishonesty once again became the monster in the room, bigger and uglier than ever. I had lost any sense of my true self through the years. Sometimes I'd get really drunk to dull the pain in my heart, and other times I would try to tell Brian how I was feeling by lashing out.

"You're too controlling. You boss me around too much. I don't like it when you leave. I'm not feeling connected. I want things to be different." I always put the truth out there, but I sometimes presented it in a way that was threatening and combative. Brian tried to recognize that what I was saying was valid, but things inevitably returned to the same discomfort and disconnect.

In some ways I had become a more confident woman since starting MM. People respected me. I changed a lot, at least on the surface. In the end I think it made Brian uncomfortable. I know he was proud of me, but I believe he didn't know how to embrace the stronger Audrey. In retrospect neither did I. I felt so weak because I couldn't control my urge to drink. To the outside observer, I was fearless. When no one was looking, I was a complete and total coward.

I was secretly and slowly destroying everything good in my life. And since I chose not to confide my weakness to anyone, no one could support me through this dark period. The truth is, there's no perfect cure for problem drinking. If there were, there would be no alcoholics, no problem drinkers, and no addicts in this world. I like the way drinking a few glasses of wine makes me feel. I like the buzz and the calming effect. For me, knowing I could look forward to the reward of a few drinks in the evening was the only way to make it through a hard day. I moved through the world at such a fast pace, my evening cocktails were the only way for me to slow down.

I didn't have a strong spiritual connection at the time nor the wherewithal to ask God for help. The only solution was to continue hiding my flaws—to deny that I had a problem. My clandestine behavior only exacerbated the severity of my drinking. The more I hid it, the more I drank. The more I drank, the less productive I was. The less productive I was, the more I wanted to run away and hide.

Until one day I did just that.

I could no longer go on with the burden of living as two Audreys.
The guilt was eating away at me. I had to tell Brian about my secret
drinking. I had to. I kept hearing "the truth shall set you free" over
and over in my head. But I hadn't the courage to face the harsh
reality of my life. I couldn't admit I had been lying to him for years. I
couldn't own up to my behavior. I couldn't fail. I couldn't disappoint
my friends, my colleagues. I couldn't come to terms with who I was,
who I really was.

No, I couldn't tell Brian. Not face to face.

My urge to flee became unbearable.

I boarded a flight from Ann Arbor to Washington. I needed the
comfort of home, of C.R. Surely he would understand. But I never
made it to his house. Instead I checked into a motel not far away
from my father's home and called Brian. On a rainy autumn day, in a
cheap motel room, isolated from the world and everyone who cared
even a little whether I lived or died, I called my husband and told
him the truth. I sat on the floor and cried. I shook so hard, I could
barely force the words out. I was terrified that he would leave me. But
I could no longer live the lie. I told Brian that I was still drinking, all
the while insisting that I was not an alcoholic. I maintained control
by the only measuring stick I had ever known, my father. I didn't
know how Brian would react, but I had made up my mind that either
he accepted my truth or I would leave him. That selfish decision
put alcohol ahead of everything that was important and precious in
my life: my husband, family, kids, everything. Everything, of course,
except my drinking. None of this registered.

Brian was quiet. He carefully and thoughtfully said he still had
a lot of concerns and fears, but he wanted me to come home to see
if we could make things better. He told me to come home. Home.
I had never understood where that was for me. I had never felt
comfortable enough in my own skin to embrace the true feeling of
being home. Safe. Secure.

I flew back to Ann Arbor and we tried to return to some sense of normalcy. We'd been saving money for several years, and by December 1999 we were finally able to afford our first house in Woodinville, Washington, not too far from Brian's mom and dad. We bought a puppy for the kids, something we had long promised them. All the moves, all the transitions from city to city, all of the displaced and unsettled feelings were behind us now. It was a new beginning. A fresh start. A life filled with hope and promise. We were living in our little world of dreams come true.

By the time we moved into our new house, MM pretty much ran itself. It had become primarily an Internet support group. People could join online and participate in meetings via MM chat groups. The media spotlight had dimmed significantly, which was a tremendous relief to me.

I was determined to stay sober this time. I had to grow up and take on my roles as wife and mother. I had to mature so I could take on my parental responsibilities. My self-defeating behavior would no longer hold power over me. My condition would not be a crutch. I took myself out of environments and situations that made it easy for me to take a sip here and there. The choices to drink, or to abstain from drinking, or how much to drink had been mine to make all along. These choices were not predetermined by a disease; they were entirely a result of my own decisions, over which I had control. I shed my "disease" and took back full responsibility for my own behavior. Once the kids started school, I began taking college classes again. I developed interests in hobbies and started to make new friends in our community.

Everything on the outside shouted, "Hooray. You're fine. Things are great." But even with my great insights, my great resolve to take control, I was still feeling empty and increasingly hopeless. I wanted to be happy, but I had no idea what happy felt like. All I knew was how to be numb.

Soon after we bought the house, I was notified that Stanford

University had received a major grant to study the impact of Moderation Management on American society. The initial finding showed that within six months of joining MM, about 30 percent of participants recognized they could not control their drinking and went on to a full abstinence program. Another 30 percent cut their drinking down and kept it under control. The final third dropped out of the program and kept drinking.

Two of the university's senior researchers were coming to interview me. It should have been a crowning moment in my life. My work was the focus and center of a Stanford University study! Instead, the night before the interview, I drank. A lot. I'm not sure why I did; perhaps it was nerves. When the researchers arrived, I was so hungover I felt physically ill.

I ushered them downstairs to my tiny home office and showed them the MM national headquarters, which consisted of an old, battered desk, two computers, two filing cabinets, and a rickety swivel chair. The researchers were so stunned by the location of the organization they failed to see that I was a complete mess. I was so paranoid they would know I had been drinking, I could barely respond to their questions. I knew my breath reeked of alcohol. I could smell it emanating from my skin. I kept my hands hidden under my thighs or in my jeans pockets so they couldn't see I had the shakes. Perhaps I'd pulled it off. Perhaps they didn't notice.

Watching them drive away, I was crushed by guilt and shame. What had I just done?

16 LaShell

DANNY BROUGHT ZACK AND ME BACK TO WASHINGTON
after Thanksgiving in 1987 so I could give birth to our second
child. Danny returned to Germany. Pregnancy was just as hard on
my body this time around as it had been with Zack. Because of my
complications, I wanted to give birth stateside to be certain I had the
best medical care possible. Zack and I moved back to Grandview to
live with my mom and dad until I gave birth. I was nervous about
going into labor, fearing I might suffer as I had with my first delivery.
I waited impatiently for the big day.

On the morning of March 15, 1988, I woke my mom to tell her it
was time. A short while later I poked my head into her bedroom. She
was still in bed!

"Mom. Get up!"

"Well, let me take a shower," she said, "and then I'll wake your dad."

I sat on a chair waiting, doing my breathing exercises as I had learned
from prenatal class, wondering what was taking so long.

Mom strolled about the house, insisting she had to make Dad a
pot of coffee before leaving for the hospital. Then she called my aunt
to see if she wanted to go with us. My youngest sister, Becki, watched
Zack so we could finally go.

"Oh, God!" I was having contractions and was in pain.

By 7:30 I was admitted to Prosser Memorial Hospital. When the
doctor came in to do his routine tests, he discovered my uterus
had collapsed. Though I was in labor, I was not progressing. I

was frightened and in pain. I began to weep, worried about my unborn child and wondering what was happening. I felt like a used car that was falling apart while everybody was trying to squeeze one last mile out of it. The doctor was afraid they would have to do emergency surgery to repair my collapsed uterus, or I would have to endure a cesarean section. I was terrified, having already been through a traumatic pregnancy and birth with Zack. The doctors came in and out of the room hoping the baby would drop into the birth canal so I could give birth naturally—but she never did.

I was desperate to be a part of this birth. Zack's birth had been so traumatic, I missed the joy of witnessing his arrival in this world. I was bound and determined not to miss the moment again. I was finally wheeled into the delivery room. I asked the nurse to position a mirror so I could watch the miracle unfold, despite my agony.

I have heard that women can become very demanding during labor, and for the most part, the doctors will abide by their wishes. I try not to be a difficult woman by nature, but I was scared and needed something for my pain. My close friend Sandy, whom I knew from church and with whom Danny had grown up, was with me in the delivery room. She helped coach me through my breathing exercises and tried to keep me focused between contractions, which were intense.

"Give me something for the pain!" I begged—pleaded—but the doctor refused. The birth was too complicated. The doctor felt he needed to know any possible complication, and so he denied my demands for an epidural.

I lay there, legs up, grimacing and pushing as the nurses tried to console me. The doctor left the delivery room to check on another patient. I glanced at the mirror from the corner of my eye and asked what the little green dot in the middle was. It was the top of my baby's head! I began to push as hard as I could. The nurses tried to stop me—they wanted me to wait for the doctor.

"No way!"

I was ready to push. I didn't care if the doctor was in the room or not. I remember seeing the doctor fly through the delivery room doors, flinging them wide open as he struggled to put his mask and scrubs on.

"Hold on, Sheryl, hold on!"

For whatever reason, that made me laugh, but just for a moment. I struggled to bring my baby into this world. I saw her tiny fingers, then an arm, and soon after, the doctor held the baby up for me to see. She was beautiful. And big. She weighed 10 pounds 7 ounces and was 22½ inches long. At that moment I thought I had given birth to another boy because of her size and muscle tone—she looked like a football player! I lay down, exhausted and exhilarated. The doctor held the baby up by one arm and leg and asked, "What do you think of your baby girl?"

Girl? Did he say girl?

One look and I realized my football player was a beautiful ballerina. I was overjoyed. And then everything changed. I heard a "plop" sound from below my waist. Nurses were frantic, yelling to start an IV in me. I was hyperaware of everything, yet no one seemed to notice me.

I was screaming, "Save my life! Don't let me die. Oh, God. Please don't let me die!" I was sitting up in the bed, yelling and crying, pleading for my life. Or at least I thought I was.

In reality I was unconscious. My vital signs were dropping. And yet I know every detail that unfolded in the delivery room that day with great certainty. I watched the entire drama unfold. I heard the doctor tell the nursing staff they would all go out for pizza afterwards.

"Yes. Yes. Good idea. I want to go too!"

No one responded. My frustration was growing by the second. Why weren't they listening to me?

Suddenly I noticed a bright light that sparkled like fresh snow in the morning sun. I felt my body ascending toward the light until I reached what appeared to be a big, puffy cloud. Jesus was standing there and he told me I had to go back—it wasn't my time. I had to go back and take care of my daughter until it was her time. Jesus spoke to me in a gentle voice. I was inexplicably calm.

"Cherish her. She will not be with you very long."

I remember His words clearly, though I never connected them until after the car crash.

I awoke, groggy and unsure of all that had transpired. But I was alive and I had a beautiful little girl I named LaShell. Her name had come to me in a dream I had while I was pregnant. Prior to coming back to Washington, Danny and I were talking about baby names. Later that day I took a nap and I dreamt that Danny and I were walking along a beach. We were kicking around shells inthe sand, trying to think of names. "Shell. Michelle. Rochelle. LaShell. That's it!" Later that night I told Danny about my dream, and we both agreed instantly. If we had a girl, her name would be LaShell.

The next day I asked Sandy when we were all going out for pizza. And I asked her why it had taken so long to find a vein for the IV and how come no one responded to me in the delivery room.

"Sheryl, I thought you were dead," she said. "You were on the bed, unconscious. You were bleeding to death. You lost an enormous amount of blood after LaShell was born. No one thought you were going to survive. But you did. How could you know all of this?"

It became clear to me that my experience that day was very different than everyone else's in the room. It was also my first real encounter with Jesus. I had heard stories about people dying and going to heaven and coming back, but I never expected that I would experience such a miracle. Though it all makes more sense to me today than it did back then, I was certain there was a higher purpose for the struggle in giving birth to LaShell. I had unshakable faith that her life, as short as it might be, would have great purpose. That experience gave me clarity and knowledge to embrace every moment we would have together as a family.

I remained in the hospital for several days until I was strong enough to go home. The hospital had some concern about letting me go, but my family convinced them they would be around to help as I recovered. Reluctantly the hospital discharged me.

About a week or so after LaShell's birth, Danny's brother died. Danny was allowed to come back to Washington on emergency leave and I introduced him to our baby girl. A week after that, my grandma died. All of the stress was difficult during my recovery, but despite that, I recuperated much faster than doctors anticipated. A month after giving birth, I was allowed to join Danny back in Germany, and for the first time in five months we were all together as a family.

We remained in Germany until 1989 when we returned to Fort Lewis, Washington, which is outside of Seattle. Danny was still finishing his tour of duty, and I went back to school to earn my GED. I tried to work too, but it was much easier for me to be home with our two toddlers. Because my pregnancy with LaShell had been so trying, when we were in Germany Danny had been adamant about me staying home and *only* taking care of our kids. Years earlier, with only Zack at home, I babysat for other soldiers' kids as a way to make some extra money. But now with two kids of my own, there was no way I could take on the responsibility of someone else's kids. I didn't have the strength to do much else beyond caring for my own family and studying for school.

Danny and I were getting along great. Our relatively poor backgrounds had taught us to save and manage whatever money we had after paying our bills. From day one everything we did, we did on our own. We did whatever we could to make sure we had a nest egg and emergency money. Automatically $200 to $300 a month came out of his paycheck and went into our savings account. We learned how to budget and not overspend, so we were comfortable knowing we'd never really be in a financial jam. For the most part we lived debt free.

We both wanted a lifestyle for our family where God was the head of the household and to live in a home where everyone respected one another. We didn't want to be in an environment where we yelled and screamed at each other or had our children heard us call each other names. Physical violence of any kind simply would not be tolerated. We aimed for a relationship where we sat down and tried to talk things out in a calm, reasonable manner. And though we had a few slips, we really tried to abide by these guidelines in our relationship.

Now that we were in Washington, we drove to Yakima to see our families as often as we could. We'd sometimes make the 170-mile trip two or three weekends a month. Danny's sister Jeannie was always one of my closest friends. We usually stayed at her house when we visited and always had a good time. Danny was close to all of his siblings, and I admired their rapport—and might have even envied it from time to time because I never was close with my sisters, though I very much wanted to be. But my sisters were basically raised to resent me. I was always the family scapegoat. No matter what happened or who did it, it was always my fault.

Despite the years of abuse and mistreatment by my family, they remain the only family I have. I have always placed an enormous value on their presence in my life. I always loved them unconditionally, even if I didn't like them all the time. I quietly carried my concern that my children would somehow endure the same miserable treatment that I did. I was fiercely protective to ensure their emotional safety and well-being, and yet I still found myself going home, subjecting myself to my family's constant abuse.

Since I was raised in a military family, I understood the pros and cons of serving in the armed forces. The Army meant stability and peace of mind. In the early '90s, the first Bush administration enacted a new military policy aimed at scaling back the military. Bases such as Aschaffenburg, where Danny was originally stationed in Germany, were either being downsized or closed. There were not enough U.S. bases to hold us, and no military jobs for the soldiers to fill. Congress, acting under the guidance of the White House, passed new legislation that would allow soldiers willing to take an early discharge to collect a hefty opt-out package. For some it made sense. For others it was a double-edged sword. For Danny it was a difficult and emotional decision.

On one hand his opportunities for advancement were diminished by the imposed choke in the promotional funnel as soldiers competed for fewer advanced ranks. On the other hand we couldn't stay unless Danny made the higher grade within a given time frame. By 1992 Danny had decided to make the Army his career. If he was not promoted, he would automatically be dropped in grade and would not be eligible for the payoff. We knew a number of friends in Germany who had already been forced out by the lack of promotions. Others were opting for the payout.

Danny and I anguished over what to do. We loved our life as a proud American military family. We honored our role and cherished our responsibilities to our country. After numerous long discussions and hours upon hours of prayer, we agreed that Danny ought to stay in the Army. Our decision was almost immediately confirmed when Danny was offered the opportunity to serve another tour of duty in Germany if he opted to go the career route.

One morning a few days later, Danny woke me earlier than usual.

"I've gone for the money."

I thought he was joking. We had agonized for months before making the decision to stay in the Army. Surely Danny knew what taking the money would mean to us as a family. It went against everything we had planned.

I didn't believe him. All I could say was, "Yeah, right. I'm going back to sleep."

"No, honey. I'm serious. I've signed the papers. I'm out."

I sat up, rubbing the sleep from my eyes, trying to comprehend what he was saying. I was halfway packed for our move back to Germany. We were about to uproot our family and now, at 5 o'clock in the morning, somehow Danny decided this was a good time to tell me he signed out.

The deal was done. There was no turning back. Once Danny signed those papers, he was no longer in the Army. He chose the money over every ounce of thought and hope we had for our future. At the time, the money seemed like a lot to a young family like ours. In retrospect I suppose it was true. However, I later learned that Danny panicked when he made his abrupt decision to sign out. He feared he was going to be kicked out of the Army and lose his bonus. Word had come through various friends and coworkers that there was a total freeze on future promotions. Out of desperation Danny did what he thought was right. He believed his decision was in the best interest of his family.

Through the years I have learned that important decisions cannot be made from a place of panic. The very day Danny signed his papers to leave the Army, military policy shifted once again. Danny would have received his promotion and his career path would have been set into motion exactly as we had envisioned. Before the ink was dry, it was already too late.

Danny's decision and independent choice changed the course of our lives. Our relationship was never the same, and worse yet, something shifted in Danny. I think his fear of appearing weak and frightened overshadowed his trust and faith in our relationship and, bigger still, his relationship with God.

As we were trying to untangle ourselves from this sudden change in plans, I received a phone call from my mom telling me that my dad had fallen ill, and she feared he was dying. My sister was about to leave for her tour in the Army, so she could not help out. Mom didn't drive and she needed to be shuffled to and from various doctor appointments at the hospital where Dad was resting. Danny and I thought it made a lot of sense for the kids and me to move in with Mom and Dad while Danny transitioned from soldier to civilian. We talked about all of the ways this might help stabilize us as we embarked on a new beginning.

A week after moving in with my folks, I discovered my dad

was suffering from diabetes—harsh but hardly fatal. The doctors explained he needed to bring his disease under control, but he was healthy enough to come home. When Danny found out Dad was not going to die, he somehow twisted it in his mind that I manipulated him to move in with my parents and away from him. He believed I was mad at him for leaving the Army and used my dad's illness as an excuse to leave. Though it's true I was disappointed in his decision, it had no bearing on my choice to help my mom and dad in a time that I believed there was critical need. I had truly believed my dad was dying, and there was no one to help Mom but me. All of my siblings were living too far from home to help.

Out of loyalty and urgency I had agreed to help, unaware of the mounting trouble my decision would make in my relation with Danny. He was not happy that I chose to nurse my ailing father over staying home with him to help him cope with his transition. The tension grew thick between us. It was clear we were headed for a fall.

17 Wide-Awake Blackout

I HAD TO FIND THE COURAGE TO TELL BRIAN I WANTED to leave him. I knew in my heart our marriage was over. When C.R. left us, one of the long-term wounds was my expectation that all men leave. I lived in constant fear that the love, affection, and trust a man offered would sooner or later be taken away. No matter how hard I tried to change my expectations, in the end most of the men in my life did leave, so I began to anticipate their leaving. The closer we grew, the deeper the bond, the more I pushed them away—virtually forcing every man I have been with to leave. It wasn't conscious. I was never aware that I was pushing them out of my life. Now the person I was pushing away was Brian.

I challenged him every chance I got—pushing him, prodding him, secretly hoping I would hit a nerve and make him want to leave me. Alcohol was my greatest tool. I knew just how to use it to drive a wedge so deep between Brian and me that it would never be removed. The crash sealed that wedge in for good.

I deeply loved my husband. There was never a doubt in my mind about that. But I wasn't *in* love with him. We were two very different people. As I saw it, when I was with Brian I became unrecognizable to myself.

I covered up how I was feeling and refused to share what was happening in my heart; no one knew the real me. I was never the person they thought I was. I never expressed my anger or spoke my mind. I was quiet, subservient, and pensive. It's painful to suppress who you really are and disconnect from your loved ones. I was unable to connect with my husband because I was so petrified he would discover I was not who I said I was. The truth was, I was a ticking bomb just waiting to explode.

I was living a lie. I should have told Brian how miserable I was. Why didn't I trust him enough to open up and just be honest from the start? Why couldn't I just be myself? I didn't even know what that was. I had lost myself. I was drowning in my sea of lies and alcohol.

I had become a closet drinker, hiding my disease from everyone, including myself. I didn't realize how manipulative I had become. Sometimes I think my lying was far more damaging than my drinking. But I also think lying about it made my drinking a much bigger problem.

All the while, I was going to my MM group, pretending I was the perfect picture of all that Moderation Management stood for. I said nothing of my continued failures. The MM program called for three days of abstinence a week. By 1996, I was drinking seven days a week. I was regularly drinking more than the allowed nine drinks a week or the maximum three drinks a day for three days during any one week. I sat and listened as others in MM discussed their struggles with staying within the limits set forth in our handbook—limits I created and was unable to adhere to myself. I felt if anyone knew the truth, it would be devastating. I didn't want to be responsible for bringing down the very organization I helped to build. How could I fail? How could I let anyone in on my secret?

As my drinking continued, my guilt intensified. It was becoming unbearable. Group meetings were agonizing hours of listening to other people freely speak about their inability to stop drinking. In MM one assessment step is to attempt to stop drinking for a full month. If a drinker can't do that, it is a sign that his or her drinking is out of control and he or she might need to enter a program such as AA. Many times I quit drinking for 30 days or more. But soon after, I always found myself binging. I could never admit that to fellow group members either. How would they accept that the founder of MM couldn't abide by her own self-imposed guidelines? If word got out, it would trigger another flurry of controversy against MM.

After weeks of growing ever more reclusive, I stopped going to MM meetings altogether. Sitting in the meetings drew my guilt too close to the surface for comfort. Even though I wasn't attending meetings, emails, letters, and phone calls kept pouring in to my home office—the world headquarters of MM. Thousands of people were reaching out to me to help them with their drinking problems, with staying within the limits. The irony was almost absurd.

I knew in my heart that I could never stop drinking. Never.

The stress was close to overwhelming. I became anxious all the time. To seek the help of a professional would be an admission of failure. I was not ready to publicly fail. Not yet.

I believe God sometimes gives us insight into what the future holds if we don't change our course. I was to the point of overdrinking more often than not drinking. Brian accepted a job working in Chicago and was regularly gone for days and sometimes weeks at a time. His absence made my drinking easier because I no longer had to hide it. Though I usually tried to avoid drinking in front of the children, any other time was acceptable. I was supposed to be abstaining, but since Brian was out of town, I thought, "I'll drink as much as I want and no one will ever know." So I drank. And drank, and drank some more.

One night as I lay on the couch I looked across the living room into a large mirror on the wall. I kept looking at myself in the reflection, trying to focus on my image, which began to appear terribly distorted. My face looked warped on one side. My nose and face appeared to be melting off my skull. It was surreal, like a Salvador Dali painting. I stood up and walked closer to the mirror to have a better look. I kept thinking there must be something wrong with the mirror. As I came closer, I could see everything was perfectly normal. I moved back to the sofa. Once again everything appeared distorted, flawed, broken. I walked back and forth, at least three or four times, trying to figure out what was going on. Was this some sort of circus mirror that somehow distorts the image? It wasn't. It was a regular mirror. No tricks. No gimmicks. It was weird. I began to freak out.

This was a premonition that my face would be lopsided at some point in my life. I didn't know why. I didn't know when. But I knew without a doubt I had just seen a glimpse of my future.

While Brian was gone I felt lost and aimless. I spent hour after hour lying in bed, staring out the large skylight directly overhead. Days melted into nights. I could see the birds turn into stars and I began to wonder if life was really worth living. What was my purpose on this earth? I knew I loved my kids. I could never think of abandoning them. But I felt emotionally empty. The only thing that seemed to numb my feelings of an unfulfilled life was drinking. I was sliding downhill and the prospects of ever regaining my identity, my self-esteem, my self were looking dim.

By January 2000 Brian was working in Chicago, following the layoff of many software engineers in Seattle. There was little local work, so he had to take the first opportunity available, and that was in Chicago. My sleeping had become erratic. I got up at 4 o'clock in the morning and began to drink. Four a.m. quickly turned into 8. The kids left for school and I drank some more. Then noon, then 2 in the afternoon. Surely by then I had drunk enough to suffer the effects of alcohol blood poisoning. In a panic I called 911 and told them I needed help. I was sick, frightened, and not thinking straight.

But when the police arrived, I had a sudden revelation that this would mark the end of MM. I refused to let them in the house. I thought it might make the news if I were taken to the hospital for alcohol poisoning. The police, however, refused to leave, insisting they had to check things out. Reluctantly I opened the door. I tried to push the police officers away, insisting I was fine. That was a huge

Washington State Patrol

The impact of the head-on collision pushed Danny's car backward about 50 feet.

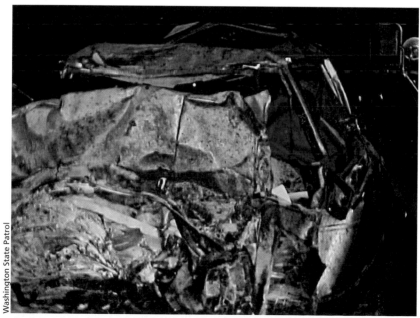

Washington State Patrol

The front of the Dodge two-door in which Danny and LaShell died: The collision crumpled the engine and dashboard into the passenger compartment.

Both vehicles came to rest facing west in the middle and left lanes of eastbound Interstate 90.

Damage to Audrey's vehicle, a Ford F-350 pickup

Scene of the crash: the eastbound lanes of Interstate 90

Audrey may have entered the interstate headed in the wrong direction at this interchange.

Audrey doing the splits at age 6

The aspiring ballerina

Audrey (second from right) with her sisters, Tina (left) and Nicole (second from left), and her mother, Christa, while living in Boulder, Colorado

Audrey when she was in her early 20s and her father, C.R.

Audrey (center) with her sisters on July 4, 1976

Audrey and Brian's wedding, July 11, 1987

Audrey and Brian during a visit to her mother in New Jersey, June 1995

Audrey with Lindsey and Samuel shortly before she began her prison sentence

Sheryl and her family outside the courthouse hold photos of Danny and LaShell during a press conference following the sentencing.

Audrey speaks briefly to the media outside the Kittitas County courthouse after pleading guilty to two counts of vehicular homicide.

Danny cooking in the restaurant kitchen the night he and Sheryl first met

Sheryl and Danny posed for this photo during their first date.

Sheryl and Danny's wedding, with their parents, May 26, 1983

Sheryl holding newborn LaShell, with Danny and brother Zackery

Danny and LaShell

A family portrait taken in November 1992: Zackery was 6½ and LaShell 4½.

Old-time photos became a tradition for the family. This one was taken during a vacation in August 1999.

The Washington State Department of Transportation and Mothers Against Drunk Driving used LaShell's photo for traffic-safety billboards.

mistake. I struggled as I tried to push the officers out the door. Before I knew what was happening, they wrestled me to the ground and I was pinned to the floor, handcuffed, with a strange man's knee against my neck. I was obviously intoxicated. The police had no idea who I was, if I might have a weapon, or if I was dangerous. They were only following protocol.

I was taken into custody and checked into a three-day rehab center to detox. Brian was still out of town. The kids went to my mother-in-law's house near our home. I spent three days drying out, thinking about my choices. It was time to tell MM that I needed to go into an abstinence program. There would be no more hiding from my problem drinking.

From: MM@Moderation.org
To: moderationmanagement@onelist.com
Subject: Announcement from Audrey
Date: January 20, 2000
Hello Everyone, fellow MMers,

I have made the decision recently to change my recovery goal to one of abstinence, rather than moderation.

As you all know, Moderation Management is a program for beginning-stage problem drinkers who want to cut back OR quit drinking.

MM provides moderate drinking limits based on research and a fellowship of members who work the program's steps together. Some of our members have been able to stay within healthy limits; some have not. Those who acknowledge they cannot stay within moderate guidelines have always been encouraged to move on to an abstinence-based program.

I am now following a different path, and to strengthen my sobriety I am attending Alcoholics Anonymous but will also attend Women for Sobriety and SMART Recovery. I am sure I can learn much from all of these fine programs.

Initial results from a National Institutes of Health-funded study on MM out of Stanford University show that indeed members of MM are highly educated, have jobs, families, and most of their resources are intact. It is also very unlikely that they would define themselves as "alcoholic" and in fact shun any program that would label them as such. But they are concerned about their drinking. They are attracted to MM because they know they will be allowed to take responsibility for making their own choice of recovery goals.

For many, including myself, MM is a gateway to abstinence. Seven years ago I would not have accepted abstinence. Today, because of MM, I do. Whether abusive drinking is a disease or a learned behavior does not matter. If you drink too much and this is causing problems in your life, you need to do something about it. We're intelligent people, but sometimes we need to quit debating in our heads and look at what's in our hearts.

If you, like myself, find eventually that you cannot stay within our guidelines, there is no shame in admitting this. In fact, it is a success.

A big success, because you have found through our program what you need to do to really live life to its fullest. As Dr. Ernest Kurtz, one of the foremost experts on AA, who wrote the foreword to our handbook once predicted, "MM will one day refer more people to AA than any other program."

He may be right!

My heartfelt best wishes to each and every one of you as you discover your own recovery goal.

Audrey Kishline
Founder, MM

In the two months that followed, I was supposed to be attending AA meetings, abstaining from drinking, and "working the program." I had huge remorse about having become so drunk and calling the police. Remorse was my motivation this time to get my act together and quit drinking. But the same old cycle I lived in for years began to repeat. I'd abstain for a few days at a time and immediately fall off. Each fall was getting worse and worse. It became increasingly harder for me to remain anonymous too. I was easily recognizable when I attended AA, which only added to my discomfort. I never identified myself as anyone other than "Audrey," but lots of people knew exactly who I was.

I was aware that Brian had placed an expectation on me to be alcohol free when he returned from Chicago. That thought scared me to death. I couldn't seem to maintain sobriety, so I faced hiding my drinking again. Total abstinence was not an option. I knew I'd go back to sneaking drinks when Brian came home. I panicked. I was scared and weak. Brian was still in Chicago so I had no reason to hide my drinking. I could get plowed and he'd never know. So I began to drink—again.

I started early that morning, March 25, 2000. I chose vodka instead of my usual Chardonnay. I needed courage to tell Brian how unhappy I was, and vodka would be the source of my bravery. The more I drank, the more I fantasized about divorcing Brian. Moving away. Living a different life. Not living a lie. I didn't want to lie to Brian or anyone else anymore. I wanted to live my life the way I was supposed to, free to be who I really was.

I didn't know I was dreaming. I thought it was real. Hard and painfully real. I was in a wide-awake blackout which quick became a real-life nightmare.

A wide-awake blackout is scary because most people don't even realize they're in one. You function and speak normally, but you are completely intoxicated and unable to make clear-headed decisions. In an instant a person can seemingly go from drunk to blacked out without passing out. You never know when it will happen, what chemistry will bring it on, or how it will affect you, but it can happen. I know many people who can't remember what happened to them after a hard night of partying. They know they went out and drank excessively, but they have absolutely no recollection of the evening's events, whom they were with, the conversations they had with friends, or how they made it home.

That day I couldn't shake my need to flee. I had to leave, get out of town, go someplace else. The walls were quickly closing in. I couldn't stay at home anymore. I decided to make the five-hour drive from Seattle to Spokane to see my dad. I didn't pack a toothbrush or change of clothes—or even my laptop, my most valued possession. I had no idea what I was doing. I didn't even know I was drunk or how drunk I was. In the past when I had too much to drink, I usually just passed out. This was a new state of intoxication.

One of the primary rules of MM is to never drink and drive. While I was in MM, I never drove drunk. I worried about being caught and arrested and having my DUI end up in the national media. When we went out to dinner, Brian always drove, so drinking and driving was never really an issue or concern. But once I left MM, it was a whole new game. I'd been lucky up until now. Sadly, on March 25 my luck was about to run out.

One of the last things I remember was calling Brian's mom to ask her to pick up the kids from school. I climbed into our big brown pickup truck. I saw my hands on the steering wheel. I checked to make sure no one was behind me before backing out of the driveway. I hate driving on freeways, especially snow-covered passes. I would have been too frightened to make the drive sober. Somehow I made it from the 405 freeway out of Seattle onto Interstate 90 toward Spokane. I drove well over 100 miles on a snow-covered mountainous pass in the fading light. I can't remember if there was snow on the roads, but I recall snow piled up on the sides of the pass.

For a good portion of the drive, I was on my cell phone. Sometime that evening I may have spoken to Brian. I can't remember for certain. But I do recall that I spoke to my sister-in-law several times, who called the police to report me as a drunk driver after we hung up the first time. She could tell I was very drunk and kept telling me to turn around. She pleaded with me to get off the highway and go home. She was telling me not to leave Brian, that I wasn't thinking straight.

"You must turn around." She was insistent.

I should have just pulled over and stopped the car.

"Audrey. Turn the car around and go home."

Those words were the last sounds I remember hearing.

My phone went dead.

Silence.

18 Unraveling

THROUGHOUT MY MARRIAGE MY MOM EXAGGERATED
stories that sabotaged my relationship with Danny. I never
understood her motivation, but the impact of her behavior on our
marriage was disastrous.

For example, I worked for Tupperware between 1990 and 1992.
In June 1991 I attended a convention in California for a few days
while Mom agreed to watch the kids. Danny was in the field when
his unit was called back to regroup for deployment during Desert
Storm. When Danny returned he phoned Mom's house looking
for me. In the rush he'd forgotten I was traveling for work. It
never occurred to me to leave a note for him at home—he was not
supposed to be back yet. When Danny asked where I was, my mom
told him I had dropped the kids off and she hadn't heard from me or
seen me for a week! Mom made it sound as if I was off cheating on
my husband when she knew I was in California learning how to
sell Tupperware.

It was absurd, but Danny fell for her tricks every time. When I
found out Danny was home, I anxiously tried to reach him. When I
finally did, he was so mad. He didn't know what to believe. This sort
of story began to repeat itself over and over after Danny left the
Army. It was clear that as a couple, we were in trouble.

After Dad came home to Grandview from the VA hospital in
Walla Walla, I stayed to help around the house. We had transitioned
out of Army housing and all of our things were in storage. In truth,

I had no place else to live. Danny and I had been living on the Army base, and we hadn't thought about finding a place of our own yet. Zack had resumed kindergarten in Grandview, so the thought of uprooting him again was terrifying. We always wanted our children to have a sense of stability in their lives. My parents watched the kids when I had to work so they never felt alone.

Danny came from Ft. Lewis near Tacoma to see us on weekends. We would resume our regular family activities as if no time had kept us apart, but Mom kept stirring the pot. She began to complain that I wasn't helping out enough both financially and around the house, but in truth I think she wanted me to stay so she could continue manipulating my relationship with Danny. To make some money I went to work as a waitress in a local diner. Whenever Danny called the house to talk to me, Mom told him she didn't know where I was, that she hadn't seen me for days. Her bizarre lies continued to chip away at whatever trust Danny still had in our relationship.

Danny and I spent six months being apart during the week and together on weekends. Over time, when we did get together, he ragged on me for every little thing. As our relationship weakened, Danny became adamant about wanting to associate only with people who were living good, clean Christian lives. He thought we needed to surround ourselves with like-minded people. Anyone who practiced things in his or her lifestyle that were not the same as the way we tried to live was not deemed a worthy friend. Danny never drank and he didn't like being around anyone who did. In his spare time he became even more involved in church and the community. He found peace and solitude in the comfort of the church.

For most of our marriage our friends came from the various churches we attended. When we came back to the Yakima Valley after living in a military community, our circle of friends became more diverse. I wasn't nearly as stubborn as Danny in believing that other people in our lives had to live by Christian faith. I welcomed everyone with open arms. Plus Danny was away from home during the week. I found great camaraderie in having friends. My acceptance of friends Danny considered sinners became an issue for him, and he would not bend his beliefs.

I often felt discouraged in our relationship. Danny was becoming angrier every time I saw him, devaluing my feelings. I remember one particular weekend I went out and bought a new cream-color silk blouse. I wanted to look pretty for him, not trashy, so I wore a camisole underneath. The blouse was beautiful and it felt so good on my skin. I walked into the kitchen wearing the new top, feeling like a queen.

"How do you like my new blouse, Danny?"

He stopped what he was doing, took one look at me, ripped the blouse open, turned to Zack, and said, "You see? Look at what kind of mother you have, son. Look at her clothes. She's dressed like …." His language was crude and insulting. I was humiliated.

What kind of man describes the mother of his children in such offensive ways? It made no sense. He constantly undermined me to Zack. He'd ask him, "What kind of punishment does Mommy deserve for being bad?" Our 5-year-old child was caught in the middle. It reminded me of my own childhood, when I felt caught between my parents and their adult lives.

As time went on Danny punished me for not being who he wanted me to be or doing the things he wanted me to do. He didn't like my friends, the way I dressed, or the fact that I worked. He despised all the things that took my attention away from him and our family. He began to bully me and aligned himself with my mom, even though he was well aware of my abusive history with her. Throughout the years he doubted my stories, saying no mother could treat her child the way I remembered being treated.

Looking back I can see that even early in our relationship Danny betrayed me by using my history against me to manipulate circumstances to get his way. He behaved that way from the beginning, but I couldn't see it—not at the time.

He often threatened to leave and take the children from me, saying things like I was "an unfit mother" and "no court would ever let a woman like me—with my history—keep my kids." These threats terrified me.

Despite our fights, Danny loved being with the children. He read bedtime stories and played games with them whenever he was home. He loved giving all the kids piggyback rides. When they were older he occasionally took them riding on his motorcycle. The kids loved Danny very much too.

Neither of us wanted to live the way we were. It was so far removed from how we saw ourselves as people and as a couple. We both knew some time apart might help us see things from a better perspective.

So in the summer of 1992 we separated. I remained living with my mom and dad while Danny stayed in Seattle to complete his education to become a licensed electrician. And for awhile I began to live up to—or maybe I should say down to—my mom's, dad's, and Danny's expectations of me. I thought since they believed I was out running around and acting inappropriately, I might as well live that way. I had spent years trying to shed my past, only to be faced with it again after I moved back home through all the lies Mom told about me to anyone and everyone. No one knew the real me.

Pain and anger were coming at me from every direction. I had willingly gone back to living the nightmare of my childhood, alone and helpless. In a moment of weakness, I found comfort in the arms of another man. That relationship brought me my third beautiful child, Cody, on March 11, 1994. Becoming pregnant brought me back from the brink of darkness. God knows my heart and who I truly am, and he loves me despite it all. Being pregnant with Cody gave me a purpose and a reason to look toward the future and see more than the bleakness and injustice I had seen for so long.

The divorce was a difficult process. Danny did everything he could to prove to the courts that I was an unfit mother. His hatefulness hurt everyone involved, especially our children, who were forced at a young age to deal with such anger. The courts disagreed with Danny's claims that I wasn't able to take care of our children, and I was granted full custody. We were officially divorced in April 1997.

Suddenly I was a single mother with three young kids to raise. I missed the feeling of family that Danny and I had built together. My only hope for survival was to separate myself from my family connections—which were both precious and toxic all at once. I had to find peace for my children's sake and for my own sake. I was having such a hard time dealing with all of the pressure. Danny was never going to see me as a decent person or a competent mother. My own mother never loved me or cared for me in a way that made me feel protected and safe.

I reached the point that I believed the only solution to my pain was to end my own life. That way all the fighting would stop once and for all. I even briefly thought that my children would be better off without me. I just wanted the pain to go away.

I swallowed all of the pain medication I had in the medicine cabinet. I chased those pills with a brand-new bottle of Tylenol and washed it all down with several bottles of beer. Had I not phoned my brother in Seattle to say goodbye, I would probably have died that day. But he and his wife figured out what I had done and called an ambulance from another phone. He kept me on the line until the police and ambulance arrived. They saved my life in more ways than physically.

As I lay in the hospital that day, I realized that if I was going to move beyond my pain, I would have to learn to live through it. Dying was not an option. It was not in God's plan. Once again I saw that part of my healing process was confronting old wounds. I no longer cared what Danny, my mom, or anyone else thought about me. I had to heal from pains largely not of my own making, but I also had to take responsibility for pain that I had caused others.

I began to think about how poorly I had reacted to Danny's leaving the Army. Regardless of how I felt of his decision process, I could now see that I made things worse by not supporting that decision. I thought about my self-destructive behavior, living at times as I thought others saw me—and so far away from how I viewed myself. My heart was full of pain and anger, and I was holding on to it. I had to let it go. The guilt. The heartache. The rage.

A heart full of anger has no room for love. Somehow in my recovery, I saw it was time to forgive—not just my mother and father, my siblings, and Danny. I had to learn to forgive myself. That was the first step. I could never truly love anyone else until I learned to love myself.

God loves me for who I am—exactly who I am. He protects me from the evil others have tried to cast upon me. I know with God's love and forgiveness, I can endure and thrive, even through the darkest moments of my life. I finally had a peace in my life that surpassed all understanding. That was all I needed to make it through.

In the winter of 1998, after a year or so of little communication, Danny and I began talking again. We eventually thought of getting back together, even though we knew it was going to be a long process. I still had a lot of work to do on myself, and for the first time I could recall, Danny admitted that he also had some things to work through for himself.

This time I never focused on his shortcomings. I stayed true to my needs and loyal to what God was telling me to do. I had learned and accepted that I could not change someone else; I only had the power—with God's help—to change myself. I never once tried to tell Danny what to change in his life. I knew he had to see it for himself and do it by himself. I had all the confirmation I needed from God that for the first time in years, I was on the right path.

After the divorce Danny bought a small three-bedroom house on Cedar Street in Grandview. It was only a couple of miles from my mom and dad's house so the kids could visit whenever they wanted. By early 1999 things were going pretty well and Danny suggested the kids and I move in with him. But I knew we needed to move slowly if we were going to rebuild our relationship in the right way, and I was concerned about appearances because we were still divorced. Instead we bought a camper-trailer and kept it on Danny's property. The plan was that LaShell and I would live in the trailer, and the two boys could have the two extra bedrooms in Danny's house.

Shortly after the kids and I moved, the company Danny worked for started working on a big construction project in Bellevue, near Seattle. He and four coworkers figured out that it would be more economical for them to take the camper to the job site during the week, live in it, and then come home on the weekends than to try to find cheap housing or make the drive every day. It made sense, and Danny moved the trailer to Bellevue. But then three of the others changed their minds and decided not to take the jobs in Bellevue. So LaShell and I moved into the house with the boys. On the weekends Danny lived in the house and I slept at my mom and dad's.

19 Prison

WITHIN MINUTES AFTER THE JUDGE SENTENCED ME TO four and a half years in prison, I was shackled, taken into custody, and led to a tiny concrete room inside the courthouse. I sat on a cold metal bench, trying to look out a small window that had been sealed shut. I looked around for some sort of call button in case I needed help, but my needs no longer mattered. The heavy metal door slammed shut, reverberating with a clinking sound I will never forget. I sat and waited. I could see puddles of old urine on the floor and what appeared to be dried vomit. The lone stainless-steel toilet was not something you'd ever want to sit on.

I wondered who had been here before me. What did they do to end up here? I convinced myself that I was not one of those people. No. This was not how I live. What if they forgot about me? How long was I going to be in this god-awful place? I sat there with my thoughts spinning faster and faster out of control. My chest grew tight with panic, which was now settling in like a bad case of the flu that lingers. A guard entered and unshackled me for an hour or so—an ironic moment of false freedom.

Several hours later I was taken to the Kittitas County Jail, connected to the courthouse, to receive my first official jail clothing. I turned over all my personal items. My pretty black suit and pumps were swapped for a baggy orange jumpsuit and orange rubber shoes. I wasn't even allowed to keep my own panties or bra. While getting re-dressed, I realized that my underwear was obviously used, very used. It was gross. For the next three days the used socks, bra, underwear, shoes, and clothes were my only belongings in the world. I now understood that prison was going to be horrible, far worse than I had ever imagined. For now, I concentrated on making it through my transition from citizen to inmate.

My meals were served on rubberized plates. They were filthy dirty—but so was jail. I was issued a tiny, scratchy army blanket so I could attempt to stay warm sleeping on a metal bed in the incredibly small, cold concrete cell. I was given a tiny toothbrush, a small bar of soap, one roll of toilet paper, which had to be turned in empty to be rationed another. If I wanted to shave my legs or under my arms, I had to check out a razor and check it back in. After my first 24 hours of confinement, shaving my legs seemed unimportant. I didn't care about anything. I wanted to die.

I spent three hellish days worried I might contract some horrible disease from the meth addicts who came and went. Those women weren't being sent to prison; they served their time in the county jail. I had never before been exposed to anyone coming off hard drug use. I'd only known alcoholics. I stared in utter disbelief at their rotting teeth, cracked skin, and open, oozing sores. I saw one woman who had shot up so many times, she had no more good veins. I went into the system a complete "germiphobe." Within hours I was eating with, sleeping near, and surrounded by diseased addicts. There was nothing I could do, so I quickly learned they were merely a part of prison life. But it all terrified me.

Thankfully my stay in jail was only three days. A lot of prisoners spend up to six months or more waiting to be transferred to prison. Because my case was considered to be high profile, I was moved through the system much faster than usual. Within days I was transferred to the Washington Corrections Center for Women, also known as Purdy Prison. Purdy had a population of approximately 1,700 inmates when I arrived there in 2000. I was taken early in the morning to avoid a media frenzy. Braces chained my hands at my waist and I was shackled at the ankles. I hobbled in my orange suit and rubber shoes to the waiting unmarked police car to make the five-hour drive to Purdy. I was buckled into the backseat, still shackled, as two female officers sat up front. A large grille separated us. I could barely move and I had to pee.

The officers ate, smoked, and laughed in the cool air-conditioning, that could not reach where I was sitting in the backseat. I was sweating profusely, though I can't say whether it was more from the oppressive heat or my nerves.

The last movie I saw before my sentencing was *The Green Mile*. This was all I could think about as the squad car drew closer to prison. I didn't know what prison would be like, but I hoped and prayed it would be better than jail. My lawyers hadn't provided me with much insight on what to expect. The chief of corrections at the county jail told me a little and gave me some good advice. She knew I was in over my head. She could tell I was not very street smart, and the inmate population would smell my fear a mile away. I would be a newbie—fresh meat on the block. She explained that prison life was about survival. There would be beatings, drug dealing, and even killings. It was crucial to align myself with the sort of people who would protect me and wouldn't hurt me in any way. She told me not to associate with anyone until I could gain a sense of who they were. She also assured me I could file a grievance if a guard did something that wasn't right or if I was being mistreated in any way. She told me not to worry, even if I had to take my grievance all the way to the warden.

A lot can happen when women are trapped in an environment such as prison. Some of the inmates were serving life sentences and had nothing to lose. If they disliked me, it wasn't out of the question they would plant drugs in my cell, snitch on me for something, and even brutally attack me—or worse.

I arrived at Purdy and was taken to Reception Processing, where inmates are initially booked into the system. I was placed in an open cage that looked no different than a standard dog cage, except this one was big enough for a human. Everyone in receiving could see me standing there, helpless and scared, shackled and shaking. There must have been a couple of hundred people, all dressed in the same khaki pants and shirts. Some called out, "Fresh meat on Pod A," referring to me, inmate Kishline. I didn't think I'd ever grow used to my new identity.

It had been six hours since leaving the jail, and I still had to go to the bathroom. I was worried I would humiliate myself if I peed in my orange jumpsuit. Surely I would not have been the first to do so, but I didn't want to start prison as the new girl who peed her pants.

For the most part I understood that the prison guards just had a job to do. To them, we were nothing more than animals they had to watch over for eight hours a day. Some were better than others, and some were purposely cruel. The prisoners could watch me from the lunchroom as I made my way from receiving into the system. Many of the women routinely watch receiving to see who is coming in. Some are expecting old friends—women who have been in and out more than once; others are sizing up the new blood. I felt like I was watching myself in a movie. One day I'm in a blackout, I drive my car, wake up in a hospital, and find out I've killed two people. Now here I am, standing alone, waiting to enter prison. It's as if someone picked me up in a spaceship and took me to Mars. I kept thinking, "This is not me. This is not happening." But it was.

I kept trying to remind myself that I had no right to feel bad about my circumstances. This was self-inflicted. Whatever I was going through, I knew that Sheryl had gone through so much more. My thoughts and worry for her well-being were always present— even before I knew her.

Processing continued to feel like a movie. I stood there while the guard pushed each finger down, taking my fingerprints. Sit this way. Stand here. Do this. Don't do that. They took my picture, printed my

ID, and clipped it on me. It was official: I *was* inmate Kishline. I *am* a convict. I *am* a felon. I will never be anything else.

I was in prison. I was one of them—one of the people I had looked at just days before and said, "That's not me." But it was me. Now it was I who had people waiting for me to be released. I had people looking at me, judging as I had from the outside looking in. Now I was on the inside, wanting, needing, hoping, and praying to get out.

Two women guards took me into another processing room, which appeared to be an old storage area. It had a shower, and the two female guards had all sorts of devices attached to their belts that looked official and intimidating. They carried walkie-talkies, and although they were not armed with pistols, I think they carried stun guns. Inmates are not informed about which weapons or devices the guards carry.

The guards told me to take off my clothes. I was pretty sure they were lesbians. I have two gay sisters, so I thought nothing of their butch appearance. But I did wonder how being strip-searched by two lesbians was really any better than being strip-searched by a man? Some guards were very professional, and others, well, they took full advantage of the naked opportunity.

Somehow one of the guards knew my sister had written a popular lesbian novel, *Claire of the Moon*. As the search began, she told me she had a long-distance crush on my sister, even though they had never met. This freaked me out. At first the guards inspected my body for tattoos and scars. I think I was the first inmate they had who came in with no body art. There isn't a lot an inmate can do in that situation. I thought that was all they were looking for. No such luck. I endured the humiliation of my first "official" body search.

The guards check every orifice, every nook, every crack, everywhere you can imagine, and some places you can't. I wasn't sure about how thorough they wanted me to be when they asked me to strip, but I knew this was serious and no time to test the limits. I obeyed their commands like a robot and shook every piece of clothing from my socks on up, showing the guards I had nothing to hide. I took my index finger and pulled each side of my mouth open for their examination. I pulled my upper lip, then my lower, exposing my gums. I had to hold my breasts up so they could inspect underneath. I threw my head upside down and rubbed my hair. I held each ear between my forefinger and thumb, and I wiggled my toes and lifted my arms.

Then they told me to squat. I was instructed to pull my cheeks open so the guards could inspect me stem to stern. They don't do a cavity search unless they have prior permission, but it didn't make the experience any less memorable. They instructed me to cough, just in case I had something hiding in my vagina—I'm told the cough would make it fall out. Of course, seasoned prisoners know ways to hide things and beat this process. For a first timer like myself, this was more than embarrassing—it was degrading. I felt naked in every way. Exposed. Cold. Lonely. Scared. Alone.

Later I discovered that many of the guards used the threat of a strip search to control the women inmates, and I endured my share. After a while the strip searches became as normal as anything else in prison. You accept being constantly degraded and humiliated. You absorb that feeling of seeing yourself as less than so much that you begin to believe it is true. You identify with those around you. By the time I left, I actually preferred the company of my fellow convicts over my former friends.

After the initial strip search I was given my prison clothes, which consisted of white shoes, heavy khaki pants and shirt, an undershirt, a bra, and some underwear. Nothing fit right and everything itched. I later learned how to cut my bra to make it fit better and more comfortably, which would have been an infraction if the guards had known. If I had gotten caught, I could have been sent to "the hole," the isolation cell. I had already heard about the hole and knew on my first day in prison I never wanted to go there.

I was taken to my 8×10-foot concrete cell in the Reception Unit of the prison. I would be housed there until the prison could decide where I belonged. The population in receiving consisted of every type of woman, ranging from women who wrote a few bad checks to the hard-core killers.

The cell had only a thin window, but at least I could see outside. The door was metal, with another small window that allowed the guards to look in every hour or so. My cellmate was working her prison job, so I was alone for a while.

Inmates in receiving are allowed out of their cells for only three hours a day. The rest of the time is spent locked up. I had nothing else to do but talk to my cellmate. She told me she was in for drugs. I later learned that the majority of prisoners were in for some type of drug-related crime. They were addicts who could not control their drug use, which led them to commit bigger, more serious crimes. They stole to feed their habit, mostly by writing bad checks, "boosting" (shoplifting), or prostitution. You could tell the addicts right away. They smoked and drank coffee 24/7. I was right there with them.

When my cellmate came in, I was surprised by how young she was. She gave me an upbeat "hello" and immediately told me she was gay. I saw she had some books; I told her I liked to read, and she offered to let me borrow some of hers.

"You want a cigarette?" she asked.

I had been an on-and-off smoker most of my life. After the crash, however, I began to smoke like a fiend. Brian hated when I smoked and told me right off the bat that he'd never marry a smoker. So much like my drinking, I tried to hide my smoking from him for most of our marriage.

"Well? Do you want to smoke or not?"

I did. Desperately. But I didn't want to start off by breaking the rules. I told her smoking was illegal. She laughed out loud and gave me the next lesson in my prison education. She taught me how to roll my own cigarettes; mine looked like a little, pregnant snake. She checked for a guard. I lit up and dunked the match quickly in the sink to kill the sulfur smell. We crouched down next to the vent under the toilet, which sucked the smoke out. I flushed the butt down the toilet as my cellmate explained that was how inmates disposed of any evidence. When the guards suspected someone was doing something illegal, they would shut down the toilet system so we couldn't flush. Less than an hour in prison and I had broken my first rule. I already had become one of "them," an inmate, learning what I could get away with.

I spent four or five weeks in receiving before I was assigned to a cell block. There were so many things I needed to learn and understand about prison life. Who is my counselor? What does she do? How do I put money on my books? How can I buy things on canteen? Did I have an appointment with a counselor that day? How would I know? If I missed an appointment it was an infraction. If I accumulated three infractions I would be sent to the hole. I also had to be sure I wore my name tag at all times. If I forgot it I'd be sent immediately to the hole. I could take it off when I slept, but it had to be on at all other times—even during surprise fire drills and cell checks.

My first day in the yard I overheard a woman saying she had a shank and she was planning to kill someone. That rattled me pretty good. I was hoping and praying I was not the target. All around me I heard about aggressive and dangerous behavior. I overheard a story about a woman who slit her own throat, a woman who sodomized her children with sharp objects, and a woman whose brother was a heart surgeon, so she cut her own husband's heart out and sent it to her brother. My head spun at the thought of being alone in this place. I knew I had to talk to someone—anyone.

I milled about for awhile until I spotted a seemingly harmless woman who was back in receiving because she had been sent to the hole. Anytime you're sent to the hole, you have to go through receiving again as if you are entering prison for the first time. She began to tell me it wasn't her fault the baby drowned. Her husband was the one who held the baby underwater. We were walking as she told me her story. Out of nowhere, I heard someone yell with obscenities, "You baby killer! Child molester!"

Was she talking to me? "Oh please, God. I hope she's not yelling at me."

I suddenly realized the woman I was walking with was the one being berated, because the guards grabbed her and got her out of there before any trouble erupted. I panicked because I had been seen walking with this woman. I remembered what the officer at county jail had told me about guilt by association—to be careful about whom I was seen talking to and hanging around with. I began to walk in big circles, pacing frantically and worrying about the big mistake I had just made.

The correctional system decides where you are sent after receiving based on a combination of behavior and the nature of your crime. Since I had no prior criminal history, I might have been sent to a minimum-security prison. Due to the felony charges against me and the sentencing deal arranged by the prosecutor, I was assigned to the medium-security unit at Purdy. I would later understand the significant difference in the two.

Being in a medium-security prison taught me the essential survival skills needed to make it through and serve my time. I learned that prison was the place to learn how to become a criminal. Many of my fellow inmates had been in and out of the system multiple times. For the most part,they were already bitter against the system. I had no bitterness, no edge—not yet. I didn't know what they knew. But I would learn, and soon I, too, would become cynical and resentful.

When I first arrived in prison, I kept photos of my children and husband nearby so I could look at them all the time. I missed them so much. I cried every time I took those photos out. My first visit with my kids was painfully hard. Samuel was allowed to sit on my lap and I could hold Lindsey's hands. I was allowed to hold Brian's hands only across a table and give him a short kiss goodbye. Seeing my son's blue eyes tear up as he waved goodbye to me was more than I could bear. He was only 8. It would be four more years before I could freely hug my children again.

It had been a little more than a month since I had arrived at Purdy, but it felt like a lifetime. The kids looked bigger, reminding me that I was missing important moments of their lives. Time was passing fast on the outside. Here, in Purdy, it felt as if it were standing still. After several months I could no longer bring those pictures out. I just couldn't look at them anymore. The children still came to visit every other week, but I could tell it was becoming hard on them too. I quit crying when they left and soon became emotionally detached from all of them altogether. I realized I had to cut myself off from the outside world—the world that cradled my children in its arms when I could not. It was too sad to think about my old life, which was gone, gone, gone.

For anyone who enters prison without an addiction, it doesn't take long for one to manifest. Coffee, cigarettes, and food are the three obvious and most easily accessible choices. Most inmates pack on a significant amount of weight their first few months inside. In my prison it was referred to as the "Purdy 30." The food is carbohydrates, served with carbohydrates, with a side of starchy carbohydrates. Eating becomes a way for addicts to satisfy their urges for whatever their drug of choice might be. As odd as it may seem, the prison food was actually better than I expected, but there were plenty of days I was unsure of exactly what I was eating.

The prison canteen offered everything from makeup to chocolate to cigarettes (for smoking in approved areas and at designated times), purchased with money held on account. The notion of having a place to "shop" was helpful to me. It was something to look forward to once a week. The warden who ran the canteen was a wonderful African-American woman who was always dressed to the nines. She wore a lot of makeup and was concerned with providing the inmates, especially the African-American ones, with makeup, hair products, and lots of other girly items. She believed it would help the women feel better about themselves. Though she offered a huge selection, it was expensive—almost cost prohibitive for most inmates. It was a classic example of supply and demand. Rolling papers and cigarettes were the least expensive. If an inmate smoked "tailor-mades," she was rich. If she had to roll her own Top, she had no money.

My time in prison was a lesson in survival. Most people inside had no money to buy their desired items so they traded favors. These favors ranged from sexual to menial labor tasks, like cleaning someone's cell or rolling her cigarettes. Fortunately my husband was able to put money on account for me right away so I could buy whatever I needed. My crutch was Top Ramen noodles soup, which I ate almost every night.

Dinner was served at 5 o'clock. I was usually hungry again by 8. I have low blood sugar, so it was important for me to eat if I felt dizzy from hunger. We were not allowed to take any food out of the cafeteria, except one piece of fruit. Inmates knew many ways to smuggle out food, even though we could be patted down and checked at any time. One of my cellmates—a large, well-endowed woman—was adept at hiding food under her breasts. She could hide half a chicken under each breast if she wanted to. She brought all sorts of stuff back to our cell. She had a rather short temper; if she offered me some of her food, I ate it, no questions asked. Out of necessity I quickly got over my germ phobia.

Inmates work various jobs and are paid for the work they do, but it's barely enough to sustain them, even in prison. At best I made $50 a month. My first job inside was working in the library, stacking books. I quickly changed to janitorial work, polishing floors and cleaning bathrooms, which wasn't considered such an uppity job.

From my arrival at Purdy, there was one particular guard who didn't like me. Maybe she had a family member who was killed by a drunk driver or perhaps she was envious of my education. I have no idea what her beef was, but she made my life very hard. She put me on the graveyard shift, which meant I worked 12 hours at night and still had to do my regular chores during the day. I had to catch a catnap here and there, being careful not to let the guard catch me sleeping when I should be awake. That would have been an infraction punishable by being sent to the hole.

My greatest fear in prison was of being sent to the hole. The hole at Purdy is a cold, tiny, windowless, noisy room. Everything is filthy dirty. You are given a rough army blanket and a rubber pillow; you lay on a rubber mattress on a metal bed. Your food is handed to you through a small 2×8-inch opening in the door. The guards never respond to any request. Your presence isn't even acknowledged. When you're sent to the hole you are usually allowed to take a shower every three days. If they let you shower, you are chained at your wrists and ankles and led to a small curtained area to shower where everyone can see you. Nothing helps pass the time in the hole. Pacing, counting bricks, humming, none of it helps break the monotony.

It was required for the guards to call for an inmate count every four hours. It is their way of checking to make sure everyone is where she's supposed to be. Inmates are instructed to drop whatever they are doing, go back to their cells, and wait to be counted. It's like taking attendance in school. Everyone has to be accounted for. One afternoon an inmate we all loved called Grandma didn't hear the call for count because she was in the shower. When she was not accounted for, the "Goon Squad" was called in. The Goon Squad guards wear black masks, big heavy protective vests, and all kinds of armament. They found Grandma in the shower, wrestled her to the floor, and shackled her. Six guards paraded this woman in her late 60s through the cell block, into the yard, and to the hole. Protocol says you are not to look at someone being taken to the hole. If she passes by, you must turn and face the other way. It was a horrible sight—one I never got used to seeing.

20 Beginning to Heal

SOON AFTER DANNY AND LASHELL WERE KILLED, THE
Washington State Traffic Safety Commission (TSC) approached me
about using their images for an anti drinking-and-driving billboard.
As heartbreaking as it was to see their faces on a billboard, I agreed
with the hope that perhaps their story would inspire people in our
community to think twice before choosing to drink and drive. I rifled
through the many photos I had of both Danny and LaShell, hoping
to find the perfect pictures.

The billboard was erected on the old Toppenish Highway, which
is a main road that leads in and out of Yakima. Anytime I had to go
someplace, inevitably I'd drive past the billboard. I blew LaShell a kiss
every day. Cody would say, "There's my sister. There's Dad." The TSC
didn't want people to become immune to the sight, so over the course
of four years, they moved it to several different locations along the
way. I think Danny and LaShell would have liked knowing they were
doing something to help spread a message of hope and inspiration.

I knew from the moment I heard the news about Danny and
LaShell's crash I would forgive Audrey. There are numerous passages
in the Bible that speak of the importance of forgiveness. I did not
want to be a roadblock for Audrey to feel unworthy of God's love
and acceptance. Forgiving Audrey was an easy decision. It was the
right thing to do.

There were times, however, when I doubted whether I was
forgiving Audrey for the right reasons. So many people thought I was

wrong to forgive her. They simply couldn't understand my need to do something like that. Their doubt rubbed off on me for awhile. That's when I asked God to guide me. I wanted to be certain I wasn't being selfish. I didn't want people to think I was only forgiving Audrey to look good in their eyes. I wanted to be certain it wasn't coming across as if I were wearing some sort of badge of honor by offering my forgiveness. That was never my motivation. I prayed on it over and over, asking God if forgiving Audrey was truly His will. The answer always came back the same. He wanted me to bring Audrey back to Him. Forgiving Audrey was my duty, my service, my higher calling.

My lawyers advised me that although Audrey pleaded guilty to two counts of vehicular homicide, I would still need to file a civil lawsuit to collect any insurance money from the crash. I was uncomfortable with that from the start. I didn't want to sue Audrey. I certainly had no intention of taking her home or money. As it turned out there really wasn't much to go after. Although I was told by several people that as a successful businesswoman and published author, Audrey must have money, the truth is, she did not. The only way I would agree to sign the legal documents my lawyers had drawn was if they could make the arrangements for me to meet Audrey face to face.

My lawyers were supportive of my decision not to pursue a financial settlement with Audrey. Although we could have gone to court and won a multimillion-dollar settlement, we all knew she didn't have the money or assets to pay it, so there was no point in pursuing legal action. Besides, money wasn't my motivation. I've lived without money my entire life. I was seeking something far more valuable than money.

I wanted to meet Audrey. Face to face. Mother to mother. I had heard her say she was sorry in court the day of her sentencing. I needed to know she was being sincere. Words are easy. Action is hard. This was my reason for wanting to see her and not just say that I forgave her.

Reluctantly my attorney agreed to set up the meeting.

I told no one in my family of my plan. I sought only the support of a few close friends from Bible study and church. I shared my quest with members of the local Mothers Against Drunk Driving (MADD) group, most of whom did not understand my need but still found it in their hearts to support me. I didn't know a lot about Audrey. I only knew what I had read in the paper and heard in court. I needed to better understand who this woman was and what had happened in her life that caused her to drive so drunk that night. There had to be years of masked pain inside her heart and soul. I felt for her. I understood she needed God now more than ever.

I did a lot of praying and fasting, hoping that God would provide me with the courage and strength to follow through. Many friends from my Bible study and church and even members of MADD prayed with me to make sure I was doing God's will throughout the process that led to our face-to-face meeting. God wanted something good to come from the deaths of Danny and LaShell. He wouldn't let them be just another statistic—two nameless, faceless victims of drunk driving. He wouldn't let them die in vain. From the moment they died, I knew there was a bigger reason to take them from me.

LaShell was too precious, too special to leave no legacy. I knew my daughter better than anyone. The moment she died, LaShell forgave Audrey. She wouldn't carry a minute, a second of hate or anger in her heart. She had such a good, pure spirit. If I dropped a glass on the floor, it was LaShell who comforted me, reassuring me that everything would be all right. When she was in the fifth grade, one of her school friends came to class in January without a coat. LaShell gave the little girl hers. She was so giving. She was my inspiration in life and now in death.

21 Face to Face

ON THE MORNING OF FEBRUARY 4, 2001, I SET OUT TO DO the unimaginable. I wasn't feeling up to making the drive alone so I asked Linda, one of my closest friends from church, and Jeff, a former policeman from my Mothers Against Drunk Driving (MADD) group, if they would go with me. Jeff actually asked if he could accompany me before I could get the words out. Both felt they had a calling by God to be with me that day. God reassured me He would provide. He would see me through this journey.

Jeff said he would drive his car. It was close to a four-hour drive from Prosser to Purdy. It was an overcast day. The sun kept trying to poke out from behind the clouds, but it never quite made it through, so there was a damp chill in the air. I never told the kids where I was going that day—only that I was taking a trip. I didn't want them to be confused or cause their heartache to resurface. The crash and loss were still so fresh. We had just gotten through our first Christmas without Danny and LaShell.

The closer we got to the prison, the more anxious I became. I wanted to back out. I couldn't think straight. My head was dizzy from all of the thoughts flying across my brain. It was too soon. It was too overwhelming.

In my mind I was screaming, "Stop the car! Pull over. I can't do this!" I begged God not to make me do this.

"Please, God. Don't make me go through with this. I know this is your will, but I can't face her. I just can't do it."

God showed me the foot of the cross. I was there, as if I had gone back in time to watch Jesus die. I looked up at Jesus. I could see His face. I could feel His pain. I was transported back in time. I could see the other two crosses and could hear people crying in the distance. I could feel the heat and the dust in the air; the smell was intense and real.

"Look at what I did for you. This is all I am asking of you, Sheryl. You can do this one thing for me."

He was right. God was asking me to bring one of His children home. How could I refuse Him? Jesus died on the cross for all of my horrible sins. Who was I to refuse Audrey forgiveness for her sins?

I needed to tell Audrey that she was not alone. I wanted to reveal God's glory and share His strength. God was working through me. This was my own lesson throughout the months since Danny and LaShell were taken from my life. This was the purpose behind all of my months of prayers. God delivered me from my darkness and sorrow.

God was in this world for both of us.

The prison was a huge concrete block wrapped in razor-sharp wire around the walls separating the inmates from the outside world. It took a few minutes of finding my deepest courage to open the door to our now parked car. We sat together in the parking lot encouraging one another that this had to be done. There had already been too much pain and suffering. It was time to begin our mutual healing. I had no way of knowing this day would set us both free. Audrey would spend the next four years behind bars, but her heart and spirit would be emancipated every bit as much as my own. It was a horrible tragedy that had made our lives collide, and the impact of the crash was much more than loss and grieving, more than bad choices. This was a seminal moment of huge eternal change.

My body trembled as I walked through the door to the prison, but I moved forward with purpose. Perhaps for the first time in my life, I knew what I was doing was right. There was no longer an internal battle. I walked with God. I most certainly was not alone.

I met Lou Delorie, my lawyer, at the main entrance to prison. Lou, Linda, Jeff, and I were buzzed into a security screening area much like the one used in airports. We all signed in. I wasn't allowed to bring anything into the prison, not even a piece of gum. I placed all of my personal belongings in a locker, then waited to be patted down by a guard to make sure I wasn't smuggling any type of contraband.

The metal detector beeped the first time I went through. I began to disrobe with every attempt to gain clearance. Beep. I held my arms straight out as the guard moved the wand up and down my body. Beep. By now the hallway was filled with other visitors and prison personnel waiting for me to get through security. For a moment I felt as if I were on my own cross. It took the guards a short while to realize that I was wearing an underwire support bra that must have tripped the sensor. I nervously chuckled, feeling grateful for the brief comic relief. I was down to the bare essentials. If I had to take anything else off, I would be standing there naked! I breathed a heavy sigh of relief as I re-dressed.

Finally we were buzzed through a large set of double doors. The doors clamped shut after every person passed through, followed by a second set of doors on the other side. Guards were stationed all around us. One set of guards stood inside a glass-enclosed booth, watching every move. Another guard escorted us through, making sure we kept to the right and stayed on the walkway. We had to walk from one building along a sidewalk to another to get to the visitors center. Every few feet we had to be buzzed through gates from one section of the sidewalk to the next. I felt like I was on my own death walk. We walked in one part through an outdoor passage lined in razor wire and mesh fencing. The sensation was eerie yet exhilarating. I knew I was only visiting. The guard explained that we were walking in a corridor through "no man's land," the area in the prison that separates freedom from hard time.

There was a mound of paperwork that had to be checked before I was allowed to meet Audrey. Every relevant prison official needed to sign off. Something in the way the warden, the guards, and the lawyers were watching me made me feel incredibly uncomfortable. They all knew I was there to meet the woman who had killed my family. I'm sure each had his or her own opinion. None of it mattered. I was more focused and secure than I had ever been in my life. I had the strength of Goliath. Nothing could stop me. I was meant to be here now.

A female guard directed us toward a room that had windows all around. I could see Audrey and her lawyer standing inside. I had butterflies in my stomach, and my heart began to race. My lawyer placed his hand on the metal handle to open the door. I felt my world stop.

I looked Audrey in the eyes. I turned to my lawyer and asked, "Are we allowed to hug?" I could see the shock in his eyes as he glanced across the room to make sure Audrey's attorney had no objection. No words were spoken. Only nods between the lawyers.

I walked over to Audrey, extended my arms toward this frail, broken-looking woman, and held her, hugged her, and softly said, "I forgive you, Audrey."

She began sobbing, falling into my arms, where she hung like lead. I thought I would have to ask for some assistance to help lift her off me. I don't believe Audrey was expecting to hear my words of forgiveness. It felt as if hours passed before Audrey stopped crying, but it had been only a few minutes.

The lawyers were seated on opposing sides of the small square table. I sat kitty-corner across from Audrey. The lawyers were there for a completely different reason than I was. They tried to take control, but I wouldn't allow it.

"I am not here for your paperwork. I came to talk to Audrey. I came here to see Audrey face to face. To forgive her." I couldn't have been clearer. Our meeting had to be face to face because mere words, whether written in a letter or spoken in a phone call, would never have been the same.

Audrey looked at me, barely able to hold her composure, and said, "I'm so sorry." I could see she was sincere. Just as I had to forgive Audrey, I believe she needed to say she was sorry. Sometimes words are devoid of meaning. The only person who truly knows what is in our hearts is God. When we are called to go before Him, we will answer for that. If I hadn't forgiven Audrey in person, I could always take it back because nobody would have ever known I did it. Forgiving her face to face held me accountable to Audrey, the person I was forgiving.

I looked at Audrey. I had things I needed to say. I reached out and held her hands across the table.

"Your sin is no worse than any other sin. God doesn't look at it that way. He doesn't grade it. He doesn't play favorites. In God's eyes, sin is sin. It is His commandment that we not commit sin of any kind. But, Audrey, I need you to know that we're all guilty of sin. That is why God sent His Son to earth to die for us."

There was an important question I needed to ask Audrey. Her answer was crucial.

"Audrey, I need to know if you believe in Jesus Christ as your Lord and Savior?"

Thankfully, she answered "yes."

Had she said no, I felt God wanted me to share with her the teachings of Jesus: His love, His forgiveness, and that He is always there for her. I needed Audrey to know that all she had to do was ask for Him to come into her life. He would never say no. I wanted Audrey to know that God didn't expect her to be perfect before she came to Him.

Audrey and I spoke for a few minutes about our children and how we were each getting by. Soon thereafter the lawyers, clearly uncomfortable with the instant familiarity Audrey and I shared, began their negotiations. I hated being a part of their conversation; I wasn't there to discuss "terms" or "settlements."

Audrey could not stop repeating "I'm so sorry for what I've done." Each time, I responded the same way: "God is the only one who knows our true heart. All I can do is follow His calling. And God is calling me to forgive you and to share with you the teachings of Jesus Christ." My heart was broken, and yet I could feel the first inklings of it mending with every moment we shared. Strangely though, I never cried.

The drive home was peaceful. For the first time in almost a year, my heart was filling instead of draining. My friends and I didn't speak much, even when we stopped for a bite to eat. There really wasn't much to say.

When I arrived home, I hugged my sons a little longer than usual. I was so grateful to feel them in my arms. I thanked God for my joy and abundance being their mom. I fixed dinner as if it were just another night. I helped Zack with his homework and watched TV. After both boys went to bed, I went to my room to read my Bible for a little while. This would be my first good night's sleep since the crash.

22 Forgiven

I HAD BEEN IN PRISON ONLY THREE MONTHS, BUT IT already felt like years. I knew my lawyer was in contact with Sheryl's attorney. He explained that in a case of wrongful death, a civil suit was part of the process.

Sheryl had filed the suit on behalf of her ex-husband, Danny, and daughter, LaShell. I had no assets. Everything I had earned from the writing of my book and through MM went toward keening MM afloat. Brian wasn't working, and the bank foreclosed on our home. We had nothing to offer in terms of assets—even filing bankruptcy wouldn't protect us. Despite that harsh reality, my lawyer informed me that a meeting was being arranged to discuss a settlement with the Maloy-Davis family. He explained that I should expect to spend the rest of my life buried in debt since the law allowed the family to file a civil suit upward of $10 million.

As far as I knew, the conference to discuss the civil suit terms would be between me, my lawyer, and the lawyer representing the family. For security reasons inmates are not allowed to know when special visits are scheduled. The purpose is to make it impossible to stage any action or escape.

On the day I found out about the meeting, I had no idea what was coming. In prison whenever a guard approached me, I froze in fear that I had done something wrong. "Now what?" I thought. Inside the system we all committed small infractions. Borrowing or loaning a cigarette, smoking in cell, storing an extra pair of underwear—it didn't matter how trivial the breach seemed, the act was against the rules. Whenever a guard approached, it meant trouble. So I was relieved when a guard ordered me to report to my counselor for further instructions.

When I arrived my counselor told me I was scheduled to have a meeting with my lawyer in the very near future, but he had decided to bar me from that meeting because one of the victims' family members had decided to come along. She pointed out that it was her belief that my court papers clearly stated I was to have no direct contact with the victims' family.

There was nothing I dreaded more than seeing Sheryl Maloy face to face. What could I possibly say to this woman to let her know how sorry I was? I could think of no better news than I was barred from the meeting. I was relieved.

Then, for reasons I still don't understand, something inside me said, "No, this is not right." Maybe it was my remorse or guilt, but something made me question my being barred from seeing the victims' family.

"I don't think you're right. I don't think there is anything that stipulates that I cannot have direct contact with the victims' family. We need to check my papers."

A frantic search ensued, and it was determined I was right. The court had not instructed me to be barred from contact—a rarity in such cases. The counselor acquiesced and allowed me to have my meeting.

The day of the meeting my heart raced the moment the guard found me, working in the library. Two officers came to escort me to a special meeting room in the visitors center, which was across from the main prison building where I was housed. My heart was beating so hard I thought I was going to die. I was led to a large concrete hall with metal tables and benches. At one end stood a glass-enclosed room for attorney meetings. Security cameras were set in the ceiling from every vantage point so the guards could watch every move, although they could not hear my conversation.

My attorney had already endured the sign-in and pat-down process. He stood in the waiting area until I was brought through the heavy double doors connecting the visitors center to the prison. We sat together discussing paperwork and settlement points, but I never heard a word. Anxiety blanked out my mind. I couldn't stop wondering about what was coming next. Who was coming with the Maloys' lawyer? My entire body was shaking in one big tremor with fear and anticipation.

And then she walked in.

I immediately recognized Sheryl's face from television and the courtroom. I was panic-stricken and horrified. I didn't know that she would be the one coming, and I had hoped it would be someone else. Anyone else.

I had no idea why she was there. Would she sit stone cold and stare me down? Would she berate me, lash out, scream, yell, cry? I had no clue what to expect, but I knew I deserved whatever wrath she threw my way.

I stood as Sheryl walked into the room. I wanted to show her respect and remorse. Sheryl was accompanied by her lawyer and, I thought, another man. I am absolutely certain she was there with two men. The other man was a gentle-looking soul I can't really describe, but I know he was there. There was a softness and comfort about him. He didn't say a word. He just sat beside Sheryl's lawyer. I would later discover two men did not come into the room, so I have no explanation for what I saw. He was not physically real, but it would turn out he was the most important man in the room.

The guard warned us of the cameras, making sure we knew every move was being monitored. He studied all of us as he backed out of the room, locking us in as he shut the door.

Sheryl wore a sweater that looked soft and warm—a far cry from my rough, itchy prison garb. She asked her lawyer if she could talk to me.

"Here it comes," I thought. The tension was building so fast, I began to feel dizzy with fear as tears rolled down my cheeks. I closed my eyes in anticipation of being called every unthinkable name. I was prepared for every horrific word, but they never came.

I watched Sheryl ask her lawyer a question but couldn't make out the words. Remarkably Sheryl walked toward where I was standing. I just wanted to say, "I'm so sorry," but couldn't form the words with my mouth.

"I'm …" I was crying too hard to speak.

Sheryl drew closer, threw her arms around me, and said, "I forgive you, Audrey." She used my name. It was so unexpected.

I could not believe what I heard. I was suspended in a life-altering moment where time seemed to stop. No one else mattered in that moment except Sheryl. She had come to forgive the woman who had carelessly and cruelly killed her child and her husband. I killed two innocent people—snuffed out their lives because I chose to drink and drive. There was no way to make up for what I had done, the pain I had caused, and the anguish I had inflicted. If I could give my life twice to this woman, it still would not be enough to assuage her loss. A harsh lashing that stripped away my skin and exposed me to the bone would have been easier to take. After all, that is what I thought I deserved. Not this. Anything but this.

What did this all mean? Was there a responsibility thrust upon me now that I wasn't prepared to endure? I couldn't believe she had forgiven me. I felt so blessed and yet confused.

Sheryl continued to speak softly. Her words were as firm as her stance. God was calling. She needed to know if I was listening—would I answer His call?

Sheryl's words resonated in the room. The lawyers sat, silenced. They were there to cut a deal, make a settlement, discuss terms of the civil case. I don't think anyone expected this, except, perhaps, Sheryl.

We hugged one last time before the guards came to take me back to my cell. The process after any time with outside contact was always the same, and I always found it humiliating. The guards led me to the strip-down room. They both watched as the senior guard ordered me to remove my glasses; show them there was nothing in my mouth; strip down in stages, shaking each item in front of the officers; then lay each article of clothing in a pile. I was ordered to bend over and run my fingers though my hair, making sure no body crevice was ignored. Then, and only then, was I clear to dress and return to my cell.

This walk back was different. I had a strange sensation of feeling … weightless. I had been forgiven by the one person in this world who I thought could never forgive me. I thought about what Sheryl said and the way she said it over and over in my mind for days, weeks, months, and years. These were not just words. She meant them deeply; I felt it.

Those first few months I was in prison, I often woke up thinking, wishing, hoping, and dreaming I was back in my old life. Then, poof! I was in prison—sleeping on a hard, metal, paper-thin bed with a mattress made from ground-up paper and a plastic-covered pillow. I became numb. But now I had been face to face with the mother and wife of my victims and was reminded that she would never have her old life back either. I lost every single thing of value to me: my husband and children, my choices; the smell, feel, and taste of my home; and all of the comforts I took for granted. I felt naked— stripped of my rights, my freedom of thought, and my dignity. But it all paled in comparison; these were tiny specks of sand compared to the mountain of Sheryl's pain. Standing there with Sheryl, hearing her tell me that she forgave me, feeling the soft fabric of her sweater as she held me—well, to be honest, it was hard. It was much harder than if she had yelled at me or shaken the proverbial finger of blame in my face.

I would spend the rest of my prison term contemplating the meaning of Sheryl's forgiveness. When I told other inmates about what Sheryl had done, their eyes teared up or they got goose bumps. Sheryl gave me the greatest gift that day—her forgiveness offered me hope. Her forgiveness is a blessing. I think it is the only reason I am alive today.

At first I made different types of calendars to keep track of the days I had remaining: one counting backward by days, another marking off the months one by one. There was a sidewalk in the prison yard where I could count the bricks, and I used those to measure my progress. I was obsessed with the number of days I had inside. Inmates with longer sentences than mine learned to avoid counting like I did. Prison is their life. But to me each day ticked off that calendar, each brick on the walk was one day closer to getting out. I never lost track of time. My son, Samuel, began keeping a calendar just like mine. Through our correspondence, we'd count my days left together. To an 8-year-old kid, 1,200 days felt like an eternity. It felt like that to me too.

Prison has a way of forcing you into a world of emotional detachment. In time I realized I couldn't bring the outside world into my heart anymore because it hurt way too much. I couldn't handle all that I had lost, even though the cause of my loss was at my own hands. Eventually I didn't care if I ever went back to my old life. The struggle had grown too hard for everyone. It was becoming harder and harder to see my husband, who was the only person who could bring my children to visit. Talking on the phone was too expensive. It cost $15 for a few minutes, and we simply didn't have the money. I wrote letters, which helped, but it wasn't the same. My children wrote me back. Sometimes I'd receive pictures and drawings from them, which made me cry my heart out. It wasn't until I had only a few months left that I felt I could start to reconnect and began to feel safe enough for all of us.

When I wasn't working, I passed most of my time reading. I liked the solitude and serenity I felt when I read. I read Stephen King, Jane Austen, Hemingway, Steinbeck, Anne Tyler, anything I could lay my hands on. I began to read the Bible too. Since I worked in the library, it was easy for me to find the good books first, so I never had a lack of reading material.

In medium security a prisoner can have a TV in her cell, but only if she's 90 days infraction-free. Though I did earn a television, I never watched. On the other hand, my cellmate loved to watch TV, especially shows like *Jerry Springer*. She played the TV a lot longer and louder than I wanted and she never wore her headset. The sound of the television reverberated off the concrete, seemingly louder than a rock concert in Madison Square Garden. I didn't want to argue with her too much because, frankly, I was afraid of her. She was known for her violent and unpredictable temper. One morning she just blew up at me. I don't recall the reason, but she was looking at me with pure hatred in her eyes. I was lying on my top bunk when one of the newer guards came around because she could hear the yelling clear across the cell block. My cellmate had her back to the window, so she didn't see the guard ask me if I was OK. I shook my head no. The guard opened the cell and made an excuse to pull me out of there, saving me from what I'm sure would have been a severe beating, if not worse. It was common for inmates to pack a sock with the padlock we used to keep our belongings locked up and whack you with it.

Prison is not a place where inmates' requests are generally taken into consideration. I was frightened for my safety, if not my life. After this incident I asked for a cell change, but I was informed by the warden there was virtually no way to make that happen. Only the longtime prisoners are allowed to change, and even then their requests are usually denied. The only other way to secure a cell change is to purposely break a rule that gets you sent to the hole. By the time you're out and go through receiving again, your old cellmate likely has been assigned to someone else. That didn't seem like an option for me, so I talked to my counselor about my situation, hoping he would understand. He was not sympathetic; he suggested I go back to my cell and make nice with my cellmate because, as he put it, "You've got to sleep sometime."

I went back to my cell wondering how I was going to live with this woman. I tried to befriend her by asking about her life before prison. She told me she was raised by a heroin addict mother who lay in bed all day. By age 12, my cellmate had been prostituted by her mother to earn money for heroin. She later began dealing guns and eventually got busted.

Though my cellmate and I never did see eye to eye, I discovered something I hadn't expected. She opened my mind to being more accepting and understanding of people. Through conversations with other inmates, I was surprised that a lot of the women inside the system were kinder and friendlier than people I had known for years on the outside. If they liked you, they would do anything for you. When I first arrived, if I had two cigarettes left, I would hoard them until the next canteen. Not these women. They would give you their last grain of coffee or share their last smoke. A lot of them, it turns out, were just like me—addicts in a bad place paying for our choices.

Later I did change cells. One of the guards we called "Shorty" took a liking to me and pulled some strings to have me moved. For a while, the rumor was I ratted on my cellmate, and you don't want to be branded a rat in prison. Lucky for me, by this time I had made a few friends who had my back, and they sent the word out that I was cool. I hadn't ratted on anyone and I never would.

23 Getting Back to Normal

ALTHOUGH I FOUND GREAT SOLACE IN MY FAITH AND much comfort through my Bible study and prayer groups, my pain and suffering were taking a physical toll. I have struggled with depression most of my life, and losing Danny and LaShell triggered some dark, morbid thoughts. I needed to get to the core of why I was allowing my thoughts to go to places I would otherwise never consider. So I sought help from a therapist who specialized in Dialectical Behavior Therapy (DBT), a treatment designed specifically for individuals with self-harm behaviors, such as cutting or suicidal thoughts.

A key assumption in DBT is that self-destructive behaviors are learned coping techniques for unbearably intense, negative emotions. Negative emotions like shame, guilt, sadness, fear, and anger are a part of life. My doctor explained to me, however, that a person who is emotionally vulnerable tends to have quick, intense, and difficult-to-control emotional reactions to situations. I have always been emotionally vulnerable, which made me feel like I was constantly riding a roller coaster that was out of control. My invalidating environment added to the severity of my psychological problems. DBT helps me balance my emotional thinking with my reasoning.

Since the crash many people, including family members, have tried to convince me that I am mentally ill. They can't understand how or why I could forgive Audrey, but I know I'm OK and it was the right thing to do. One of my nephews asked me once to help him understand how I could forgive "the lady that killed [his] cousin and uncle." My mother answered before I could speak. She calmly explained the importance of acceptance and moving on. I was dumbfounded but relieved. I never thought I'd hear my mom say anything that was rationally kind about Audrey. My forgiving Audrey, accepting her for who she is, the way she is, and everything about her, had the unexpected benefit of helping my mom find peace and comfort. I had waited a lifetime to do something good in my life that would help my mom, and this was it.

The mother of Polly Klaas, the little girl who was brutally kidnapped and murdered in northern California in 1993, once said, "A heart filled with anger has no room for love." She is so right on. With anger and bitterness, what do you have left? Anger and bitterness. I was so afraid that my sons would spend their lives being angry over their loss that I had to lead them by example. There have been moments of anger and sadness, times when I feel angry that Danny isn't here to help me raise the boys and angry that he and LaShell are gone. Then something strange happens. When I begin to let my emotions go to a dark place, I can smell Danny coming home from a long day at work. It's a mixture of his sweat and cologne, and I know that's Danny coming around to comfort me. I also feel his presence whenever I'm seeking answers to problems I'm having as a single parent. I have found that many people view death as cut-and-dried; they like to see death as easy, as burying your loved one and moving on. I've even had people question my need to visit Danny and LaShell's grave site. But it is hard for me to accept that it was their "time" to go. I know God has a bigger plan than we can sometimes understand, so it helps me to visit their graves.

I try to live my life coming from a place of love and understanding. I'm living a different life than I had planned and it's often bittersweet. But I have to go on without my precious little daughter and without the father of my children. Parents are not supposed to bury their children; it goes against the natural cycle of life. Losing LaShell hasn't been easy, but in many ways it set me on a path of finding a different kind of strength than I ever expected.

I've gone back to school to become a paralegal. I am also considering studying drug rehab so I can understand addiction. All these fields have become of great interest to me after dealing with the aftermath of the crash. I always wanted to go to college but never had the chance, and more important, I could never afford to pay the tuition. Danny and I were so young when we married. I needed to work to help support our family. Although I loved working in restaurant management, since Danny and LaShell died, I can't seem to focus in that hectic environment the way I used to before the crash. I'm just not the same person I once was.

I know that life is a long journey, and I'm rebuilding my strength by drawing from my day-to-day experiences since the crash. It's a process. Some days are better than others. But it's important for me to be strong and emotionally together so I can help my sons deal with their own trauma and healing. I want to help them rebuild their lives while they're still young enough to emotionally grow and heal. I try to provide the type of unconditional love I craved growing up. To be honest, the kind of love I still wish for every day.

I would love for God to bring me a man who could love me and my boys. I have spent a lifetime looking for someone to love and accept me for who I am, someone who doesn't want to change me, and I still want that. I even bought a new home with the hope that God would someday add to our family. My family is wrought with challenges, so until the right man comes along, I will continue to hold my family together as both mom and dad.

Zack, who is 21, is pretty much on his own these days. He works and goes to school part-time. Cody still enjoys being home with me. A while back, he and I were talking about what he wanted to do when he grows up. I asked if he wanted to get married.

"Yup."

I said, "Do you think you'll move out of the house and live on your own?"

He smiled and said "Nope."

"Well, what about your wife?"

In his typical, I've-already-got-it-all-figured-out style, Cody responded, "We'll just add another room to the house for her!"

I had to laugh, but his conviction warmed my heart.

A few weeks later Cody and I had an argument over his video games.

"I was going to live with you forever, but you can forget it now. I'm moving out!"

I was still able to laugh.

It's so nice to know that my kids are no longer in such unbearable pain. As a parent, there is nothing worse than losing a child. Second to that is watching your children suffer. Both of my boys have dealt with their pain in individual ways. Zack has shut down and has never shed a tear. We hardly ever talk about how he felt losing his father and sister so many years ago. I have encouraged him to seek counseling, but as any parent of a teenage boy knows, you can't make him do anything he doesn't want to do. Cody has a resilience I admire. He has some focus issues, but for the most part life goes on.

When I look down the road at my future, I see a successful woman. I see myself as someone who used the tragedies of her life to help and inspire others through their own hard times. I am feeling better about myself with every passing day. I'm walking a path of learning to be at peace with myself and the decisions I have made. I have accepted the wrongs I've done and have moved past them. I refuse to let anyone or anything hold me back. I want to be around to watch my children grow to be well-rounded, happy men.

For me, all things are possible through Christ who strengthens me. No matter what happens in life, I now know, without any doubt, that you must keep seeking and searching for ways to make it better, to overcome life's challenges. If you're feeling trapped in life, pray to God for answers. Start looking around for ways to change your circumstances. As a child the only hope I had was that God would rescue and protect me, and God continues to rescue and protect me and show me the way. His way. He guides me down the right path so I don't have to worry about making the wrong choices and doing things I'll regret. Regret is a wasted emotion. If I changed one thing about my past, I would not be right here, now, in this moment.

There is a light at the end of any tunnel. You might feel like you're in a deep pit that you'll never find your way out of or feel pain from whatever trauma you've been through, but the anger, frustration, and bitterness you're feeling toward other people can be released—if you forgive. Holding on to that rage blocks you from God. He will never block you from His life, but He wants you to come to Him from a loving place. Forgiving doesn't mean you have to become friends or bosom buddies; it simply means you must release the bondage that the anger, frustration, and bitterness have created. You will never be free from that bondage unless you learn to forgive.

The Bible says "Get rid of all bitterness, rage and anger, brawling and slander, along with every form of malice. Be kind and compassionate to one another, forgiving each other, just as Christ forgave you" (Ephesians 4:31, 32).

I am very lucky that God gave me the ability to obey Him and forgive Audrey. An unexpected friendship grew from that forgiveness. I don't look at Audrey and see a murderer. I see a woman who had a lot of things go wrong in her life. I see a woman who, like me, has made a few wrong choices along the way. I see a woman who needed Jesus in her life. Audrey is a caring person who longs to make her own life a success. She craves having her children back in her life. She is a genuine friend who can call me anytime to talk about anything, and I will always be there to listen.

24 Freedom

I BUILT A SURPRISING CIRCLE OF FRIENDS IN PRISON. MY nickname was either "The Librarian" or "The Senator" because I looked smart in my glasses. Mary Kay Letourneau, who was also at Purdy when I was there, always wore super-red lipstick so we called her "Red Lips." There was also Laurie, who we called "Topster," because she was the master at rolling Top cigarettes. And a woman we called "Cup O' Noodles" and a few others. I was surprised by the depth and quality of these new friendships. I didn't expect to meet women in the system with similar interests. We were all readers and hated watching TV. Cup O' Noodles was one of three women I befriended who was serving 20 years. Despite her term she was always happy; her sunny disposition could put a smile on anyone's face. For about three months we spent all of our free time together. We all had our problems, but for awhile we had each other.

I have a chameleonlike quality that lets me fit in wherever, whenever, with whomever. I've always been interested in what makes people tick, and I wasn't afraid to ask the hard questions. I wanted to know why they were sent to prison and what circumstances in their lives brought them there. I felt their pain and sorrow and all they had gone through on their journey leading up to prison and then in prison. Eventually my heart connected with a lot of these people on a level I had never before experienced. The emotional connection was so strong and inviting.

Some women were in prison because they did the time for crimes commited by their boyfriends or husbands. Some women were guilty of their crimes and were clear about what they had done. Still others were pathological liars. They were so convincing, it was hard to tell what was real and what wasn't.

I realized that prison had an odd effect on me. In many ways it emancipated me. In a funny way I found myself while I was in prison. I had spent years suppressed and living as someone I barely recognized. I was uncomfortable and gradually becoming more distant from Brian, my family, and my friends. I was not myself. I could never tell Brian how I really felt or what I was thinking—not ever. Looking back, of course, I can see that is why I was hiding my drinking. I was hiding everything, so how could he know who I really was?

Only now do I understand that I had a different personality than he ever knew—I thought differently than he did. For one thing, I have a fun sense of humor and like to joke about things some people might think I shouldn't joke about. I felt I had to edit every word I said with Brian. He and I disagreed about everything from politics and religion to gay rights. Everything I said, every opinion I had was shot down. That relegated our conversations to weather and nonemotional issues, which didn't leave much room to talk about anything of significance.

Eventually I just quit talking. I became passive and submissive, two qualities that took away all of my inner strength. I was completely shut down—but I didn't know it. I was trying so hard to please my husband, I forgot about what made me happy. I grew up in a family where being different was great, but Brian didn't like "different." He grew up in a rigid military family where everything had to be just so.

Prison gave me the opportunity to reinvent myself. All of a sudden I could be anybody I wanted to be. I could be like Cup O'Noodles, fun, happy, enjoying life no matter how things were going. I could be like Sheryl, full of faith and love for God. I could swagger around like some of the girls in prison and develop my own funky walk if I wanted to. I became a sponge, soaking up all of the qualities of the women around me. Life doesn't sink any lower than being in prison, and yet, being inside actually set me free because the person I really am emerged with the freedom to just be myself.

I was a pretty good liar before I went to prison. Three years behind bars taught me to perfect those skills. You have to lie in prison to survive. No one moves through the system telling the absolute truth all the time. If you did, you would find yourself considered a rat, which meant being in the hole all the time or living in fear of being beaten to a bloody pulp. My fellow inmates knew when I was lying, mostly to the guards, so I could maneuver through the system.

But I stopped pretending about myself to myself while I was in prison. There was no reason to keep up my charade. I no longer wanted to live a life of lies about myself. For my kids' sake, I desperately wanted to finally come clean and live an honest, authentic life when I was out. I'd spent too many years not knowing the truth myself, so for three years all I could think about was how I wanted to change my life so I could be happy.

I made a lot of good friends in prison. I think it was because I was authentic for the first time in my life. I was as real as could be. I had nothing left to lose.

August 7, 2003 —I will never forget that date. My last day in Purdy. In the end I served three full years in prison; the remainder of my sentence I carried out in a work-release program where I was on parole until August 2005. My last 10 days in prison brought an unexpected spiritual peacefulness. Some people describe their last days as being torturous—as if the end will never come. I didn't feel that way. No, I felt very much at peace with myself. I had all of my belongings boxed up and was ready to go at 8 o'clock in the morning on the day of my release. Brian and the kids came to pick me up. I was free. I knelt down to hug my children. I held them so tight.

I stood up, hugged Brian, and asked him to take me home. We climbed into the car and drove away from the prison. I never once glanced back.

Everybody forms some idea of what she want to do when she first walks free. My wish was to go to Starbucks. I had been drinking freeze-dried Folgers coffee for the past three years and I wanted a good strong cup of joe. Brian, the kids, and I walked into the local Starbucks. I was completely overwhelmed by the sounds, the people, the aroma. All of the knickknacks on the counter, the pastries, the food, the drink menu, and the sounds of the coffeemakers, the milk steamers, the blenders—it was complete sensory overload.

I went into a walking daze, feeling like someone who had just landed on planet Earth for the first time. I forgot how to order. I hadn't seen money in three years, so I forgot about using real cash to pay for something. It was way more than I was capable of handling. Yet I was so happy to be out and free, free to be with my kids and to breathe fresh air and walk freely without anyone telling me where I could or could not step. We walked outside, coffee in hand. I knelt to the ground and firmly placed my lips on the sidewalk.

"Thank you, God. I'm free!"

Samuel seemed confused.

"Why did you kiss the sidewalk, Mommy?"

"You've got to kiss the ground when you get out, Sam." I was overwhelmed yet overjoyed.

Lindsey understood my need to kiss the ground. I tried to keep the conversation light, but she knew what the situation was.

It was a pleasant enough drive home, but in the back of my mind I knew my marriage was over. This was all for the children. I wanted to try to make my transition out of prison easy on them. I knew the past three years had been hell on all of us, but I had no way of knowing just how damaging those years were, especially on my children.

We drove to my mom's home in Happy Valley where we all gathered for our first family dinner in years. Hearing all of the clanking metal and glass was startling to me. I had been eating with plastic utensils, and the sounds of a normal dinner were odd and unfamiliar. I couldn't believe how noisy it was.

At first all I could talk about was being in prison. The stories were interesting, I suppose, and I tried to keep them light. In retrospect I think they must have been unsettling too. I was unsure of which parts of prison I wanted to share with Samuel and Lindsey. I had a need to get my stories out of my system—a need to purge the last three years as fast as I could. Talking about it, on any level, helped.

I turned to Samuel and began talking about how bad the prison food was. "The food is so bad, I'm not even sure it was real food," I said. "Beef was always served with gravy, which hid the slightly green hue in the meat. I called it 'mystery meat.'"

Samuel laughed. "Tell me more."

"Every time I left the food hall, there was a chance I would be patted down for contraband. Guards stood by the exit and randomly pulled inmates from the line and patted you all over your body to check for knives or food, which we weren't allowed to take from the hall. Even though the knives were plastic, some inmates figured out a way to sharpen them and use them as weapons."

"Did you ever take anything from the food hall, Mom?"

I thought for a moment. I didn't want my son to think I was a thief, but I also had a newfound commitment to honesty.

"Yes, I did. I have low blood sugar, so sometimes waiting to eat my next meal was very hard for me. I even blacked out a few times from my sugar imbalance. So I took sugar packets. If I had been caught, I would have been infracted, which meant I would have been in very big trouble."

"Did you ever get caught?"

"No, but I almost did. I ran out of sugar and suffered a bad attack one afternoon. I knew I had to take more sugar later that night at

dinner. Usually the salad bar just had iceberg lettuce, but on this
night there were cherry tomatoes. It was a wonderful treat. I could
see the guards were being especially thorough when inmates were
leaving the hall that night. I carefully placed several sugar packets
inside the soles of my shoes. I had to walk very softly to make sure I
didn't break open the packets. A guard pointed at me, gesturing her
finger for me to walk toward her. I was so scared. Just as I made my
way out of line, a large black woman who was also being checked
raised her arms and out fell dozens of cherry tomatoes! They went
rolling across the floor of the hall like red marbles."

"That's hilarious!"

"Well, that woman got into big trouble, but I was spared because
in the confusion of her dropping the tomatoes, the guard just waved
me through without being checked."

When I finished, there was an awkward silence, and I could
see the discomfort my stories were causing Brian. Then someone
mentioned something about the weather. I sat back and reflected
on the situation. For so many years the conversations around our
family dinner table had been insignificant, distant. We never talked
about important things; we never debated world issues or family
problems. No, we always talked about the weather, carefully avoiding
the obvious, painful truths in all of our lives. All of us had secrets,
but none of us wanted to admit them. It could not have been more
ironically different from prison, where all of us girls shared our
deepest, darkest secrets.

Weeks went by before anyone asked how I was coping, and I could
sense their disingenuous tone when they did ask. In a perfect world,
I think they would have liked to pretend that I hadn't gone to prison.
That I hadn't killed two people. That I wasn't on parole. How was I
coping? I wasn't. Life on the outside was hard.

25 The Nut Farm

ACCLIMATING TO SOCIETY AFTER PRISON WAS A LOT
harder than I expected. One of my counselors in prison explained
to me that it can take up to six months for every year served to fully
reenter society. I definitely wasn't ready to jump right back into my
family life. I was mentally incapable of being the kind of parent my
children wanted and needed. I also knew I could never be the wife I
once was for Brian. For everyone's sake I needed a place that would
give me time and space to build my self-esteem back up. Instead of
serving my parole at home, I entered a work-release program that
required me to live yet again with three women in a small room. This
option gave me a much-needed transition to think about my future
without the pressure of being a full-time wife and mother.

I had to find a job within my first 10 days or face going back to
prison. My first job was selling window shields in Spokane. Since
I couldn't drive I had to take the city bus to travel to and from
work. I had never ridden a bus before, and I was unfamiliar and
uncomfortable trying to navigate Spokane via public transportation.
The bus depot was in a very bad section of town, which meant I had
to walk alone at night through dark streets back to my unit. The
commute was very scary.

By work-release standards, my job was considered a good
one. For me, however, it was torture. It was a high-pressure sales
job—something I never had a knack for—and it required me to use
the same sales line over and over. I was always afraid of losing my

job, and if I were fired, I faced having to go back to prison to finish serving out my term. I still had to deal with the infraction system and could be written up for a variety of reasons, such as if I was a minute late, missed my bus, or didn't perform all the duties required. I panicked from the pressure and suffered full-blown attacks on a daily basis. I was not allowed to take any type of medication to help balance my blood chemistry, which was clearly out of sync, as I had to live drug and alcohol free until I was done serving my sentence.

Everything began crowding in. I felt claustrophobic, stuck, and unable to breathe. I couldn't handle the simplest task, such as opening a bank account so I could deposit my paycheck at the end of every week. I walked into the bank one day absolutely convinced the people inside would recognize the jacket I was wearing as prison-issue garb. I watched the bank security guards scrutinize my every move, wondering if I was going to rob their bank.

Now back in the real world, I walked past liquor stores, tempted by the thought of drinking but unable to partake for fear of going back to prison. There was no lack of desire, only fear of getting caught. Every day I saw people with problems just trying to get by. I was one of them, yet I was not, for I was still a prisoner, not a free private citizen. Before and after work I was required to do chores at the unit where I lived. Sometimes I would wash dishes, clean bathrooms, whatever job was assigned to me. In addition I was required to take support group classes several days a week. My life became a juggling act with too many balls in the air. It was only a matter of time before one or all of the balls fell.

I spoke to my counselor every day to explain I needed medication to get me through my daily tasks. I faced the real possibility of having to go back to prison to serve the rest of my term because I wasn't coping. In theory the work-release program is designed to help an inmate prepare to reenter society, but the reality for someone like me is that it was a lot tougher than I expected.

The time served in work release went toward serving my full

sentence. The system is built on "good time" served, just like prison, so the rules were endless. My room had to be spotless, and I shared it with others who were not as clean and tidy. My shoes had to be perfectly lined up. If they found a tissue left in the wastebasket when they did their rounds, someone would be blamed. I could not lie down on my bed during the day (unless I worked a night shift), and I could not be more than a few minutes late for any class or meeting.

Plus there was endless paperwork. I had to fill out schedules for every minute of every day. I had to identify which bus I would be on, where my job interviews were, what time I had appointments—every second of my life had to be accounted for. The paperwork had to be signed by a counselor a few days ahead or I couldn't keep my appointments. And if my schedule changed after I submitted it for that period? Too bad. Minor things like this could get me tossed out.

I could not stop to go to the bathroom or go into another place like a coffeeshop while job hunting. We were often followed by hired college kids or one of the guards to see if we varied at all from our schedules. Every job detail in the work release (vacuuming, cleaning in the kitchen, the laundry) had to be signed off by staff. And if the staff weren't available? Too bad again!

Since there were both men and women in the work release, there were a lot more rules. Men and women could sit at the same table but not next to each other, only across from each other. You had better not be seen talking to the same person of the opposite sex too long or you would receive a warning. I could hardly keep up with all the rules, even though it was like that for everyone.

If I was written up for an infraction of any kind, it worked against my time served, meaning I could lose the privilege of being in the work-release program and have to go back to prison. If I went back to prison, I faced another year and a half inside. By this time I clearly understood Purdy wasn't where I wanted to be, yet I couldn't seem to make the work-release program work for me either.

I spoke to some of the other inmates about it. They knew of only two ways to get out of work release. One was to directly threaten an officer, which meant I would lose some of my "good" time served and at the least my parole would be lengthened or I'd be sent back to prison. The other was to pretend to commit suicide, which could also land me right back in prison if they thought it was faked.

I didn't want to do either, but desperate times called for desperate measures, so I chose the fake suicide. I didn't want to do any permanent damage to myself, so slitting my wrists was not an option. I chose to put a plastic bag over my head and pretend to suffocate myself. I hoped someone would find me before I actually succeeded in killing myself, but in a way, I was so miserable, I don't think I cared much if anyone did or didn't. I lay on the floor of my unit, making sure my feet were visible, tied a plastic bag over my head, leaving just enough room to breathe, and was able to quickly close off my air supply as soon as I heard someone coming. My breathing almost immediately foamed up the inside of the bag, and my heart pounded in anticipation of getting away with my false suicide attempt and terror.

Luckily I was found by a fellow inmate before I really did any physical damage. I was in such shock from what I had just done, I began to shake and cry. Paramedics were called in, and they were required by law to take me to the local hospital. I was told that everything was going to be OK. Mission accomplished.

Not so fast.

As soon as I was given a clean bill of health, I was informed I'd be spending a little time in what the doctors referred to as "Tech," but I would soon discover it was what prisoners called "The Nut Farm." I had sunk to the lowest of lows. The only place worse than prison is the nuthouse in prison. I was institutionalized with 25 women who were genuinely crazy. I recognized a couple of the guards, who seemed more than a little surprised to see prisoner Kishline in Tech. I was actually relieved to be there because my therapist put me on medication. Thank God, I had only a few months left to serve before

I would be officially free. I began to level off emotionally and felt stabilized for the first time in years.

My first two weeks in Tech were spent locked down in my room. I was not allowed to leave my tiny space at all. I exercised by walking back and forth, back and forth, back and forth. Somehow I was able to calculate how many rounds I had to walk to cover four miles a day. I used to do the same thing in Purdy, so I had a good gauge to figure out mileage. The door to my room was all glass so the guards, doctors, and even other patients could see in at all times. Everything I did was supervised 24/7. I had to ask permission to obtain a piece of dental floss from a guard if I wanted to floss. Toenail clippers were given only if you agreed to clip your toenails in front of the guard and immediately turn them over when done. I was not allowed to have anything I could conceivably use to harm myself.

At one point I was allowed a couple of books to read, but for the most part, I spent those first two weeks alone, isolated and feeling like I was back in the hole at Purdy. Time in Tech was actually considered worse than the hole, but not to me. It was better than selling window shields.

Once I was out of isolation, I was moved to the main section of Tech where I was assigned a roommate for the duration of my stay. I was quite concerned about whom I would be paired with, as I knew there were some dangerous women in this place. There was a woman who tried to kill her own two kids in a park, a woman who doused herself with lighter fluid and lit herself on fire, a woman I had met in Purdy who cut her husband's heart out with a knife, and a mentally retarded woman who accidentally burnt down the halfway house she was living in, killing several of the other tenants—the list goes on and on.

I was eventually paired with a young woman who thought she was someone else. She was probably in her mid-30s but insisted she was only 21. She was in prison because she had used state funds to go back to high school—as someone other than herself. I knew she was a pathological liar, yet I found myself often being sucked into her stories because she was so convincing and passionate about her make-believe "life." I became fascinated by her ability to explain everything in such vivid detail. I began taking notes, trying to find the flaws in her tales. The more she spoke, the more I bought into the possibility that what she was saying had the potential to be true.

Thankfully, I realized the more she told her stories, the looser they became, until I finally figured out that she was lying about everything. It was a relief when I discovered this because I really was wondering about my own sanity.

Even though most of the women in Tech were certifiable, every now and then, one or two would have lucid moments, as if they were connecting with God or some higher spiritual place. They would begin to ask me questions that were pertinent and thoughtful—things I needed to start thinking about.

Out of the blue one day, a girl asked me, "Audrey, do you really believe you should get back together with your husband when you get out?" I was floored.

"Are you going to drink again when you get out?" Her queries caught me off guard. They were important questions, ones I had yet to explore the answers to. In some ways, because of their lack of any type of emotional filter, the women in Tech could be much more honest in how they moved through the world. They had nothing to lose. Most of them would be there for the rest of their lives. I was there for only five weeks—five very long, very hard weeks.

When I was released from Tech, I was sent back to live in the same work-release house. Once again I had 10 days to find a job. Despite the requirement to find a job after prison, few prisoners receive any employment-related training in prison. Therefore the options are narrow when they are out. Finding and maintaining a job are critical to the success of a prisoner reentering society. Research shows that steady employment lowers the rate of criminal activity after prison, but it's a catch-22. You have to land a job, but you have no experience and no one wants to hire a convicted felon even if you do.

Every time I filled out a job application, inevitably the dreaded question came: "Have you ever been convicted of a felony?" In my quest to live an honest life, I found myself checking the "yes" box. My job choices were limited, and there was a lot of pressure to fulfill those requirements—more than I was ready for.

My morning started the same every day. I read the morning paper, circled the appropriate classified ads, made some calls, and went on at least six interviews a day. I was finally offered a good job in a high-end cooking and kitchen store by a woman who admitted she had never considered hiring a convicted felon. For whatever reason, she decided to give me a chance. Even though I had to commute two hours by bus each way, I was thrilled for the opportunity.

It was a large store, where I worked side by side with 17 other women who all dressed to the nines. This was my first job that required me to dress up for work. I discovered you can actually dress pretty spiffy on a budget by shopping at Goodwill. I tried to fit in, and for awhile I was happy just to have a job.

In addition to having to work, I attended daily mandatory AA meetings and other group therapy sessions deemed appropriate by my parole officer. My day began at 5 in the morning and ended with me collapsing from pure fatigue at 11 at night. The grind was exhausting. It didn't take long for my body, which was much thinner now than before I entered prison, to give in to the long hours and lack of sleep. My exhaustion from what I thought was only a bad cold turned into a severe case of pneumonia. I became tremendously weak, eventually reaching a point where I simply couldn't pull myself out of bed. Rain or shine, in sickness or health, I was required to show up for work. My already heightened anxiety grew worse and worse, until one day I just fell apart.

I gave in.

I gave up.

I drank.

I had been out of Tech only three months to the day. The facility I was living in was one of total sobriety, so I had broken the most important rule and condition of my agreement to be in this house. I drank only a few times before I called my parole officer and confessed what I had done. I was always careful to drink only with other people on parole who were also breaking the rules. I knew a lot about alcohol, how long it stayed on my breath, and how long I would appear intoxicated, and I counted my drinks to make sure I didn't overdo it. I explained to my parole officer that I felt I couldn't handle the pressure of being out.

I also drank because I realized my relationship with Brian was really over, and I panicked about where I would live and who would look after the kids. I just lost it. I didn't care. It didn't matter if I went back to prison. I didn't mind if I ended up on the streets. I couldn't take the pressure that was building in my head. I felt completely beat up by the system. As hard as prison and work release were, at the time it seemed easier than trying to make my marriage work.

To some degree being in prison was easier than being on parole. I never had to make a decision on my own when I was inside. For three solid years my brain was in neutral. Outside, I felt like an engine that hadn't been started for years, and I was having a hard time switching my brain to the "on" position. Like anything that gets neglected over a period of time, I simply didn't function as well as I used to. I had to change my life to better, but I wasn't equipped to do that yet.

Luckily my parole officer spared me the hardship of going back to prison. I was sent to Oxford House in Portland for another chance. The program is run by the women living there—not guards. It was a normal-looking house, but there were still rules, which were mandated by the women in the house. I had to be tested for drugs, maintain a job, and participate in housecleaning chores. I enjoyed some of the women, but most of them immediately viewed me as a threat and made it clear they didn't want me to be there. They were mean and made life difficult for me, constantly setting me up for infractions I did not commit. Something as small as not putting my coffee cup in the dishwasher or leaving a hair in the tub after a bath or shower was good enough reason to be written up or "infracted." Their primary goal was to send me back to prison. They tried to accuse me of using drugs, and dried toothpaste was assumed to be crystal meth. Such constant threats became too real.

I began to panic again about losing my job and going back to prison. I hated being in the facility and I hated the women and how mean they were to me. I hated my life. So once again I became so fed up, I just threw in the towel. My history has always been the same: After a long period of abstinence, I blow it. I wanted to drink myself to death, and this time I meant it.

I packed a bag and went to see a man I met through work release. He had spent 16 years in prison for robbery. We started out as friends, but something more developed. He genuinely cared about my well-being, and I could be myself around him. He never judged me or made me feel "less than" because of my checkered past. I told him I was going to flee the country and live in Mexico. At that point I didn't care about breaking parole. I didn't care if I ever saw my children again. I didn't care if I lived or died.

26 73 Days

RUNNING AWAY TO MEXICO WAS AN INSANE IDEA. I had no money. I didn't know how I would travel there, if I would make it there. A guy I met one time in an AA meeting offered to drive me, but I didn't know him well enough to take him up on it. I'm not street smart. I don't speak Spanish. I had never lived on my own. What was I thinking? If I fled, I never would survive. Knowing all of that, I still felt like I had to escape from there.

My friend listened to me rant, insisting I was really going leave, then he did me the favor of a lifetime. He knew the system, and he knew I was about to make a mistake of colossal proportions. I finally calmed down long enough to agree to join him for a hamburger. I didn't know it at the time, but it was a setup. We were in the diner when I heard a voice from behind ask, "Are you Audrey Kishline?"

My heart sank. This was the moment I had dreaded most since I left Purdy. I was going back. I was going back to prison. My life was over.

"Please step outside, ma'am."

I slowly stood up from the table, feeling as though I was outside my own body watching this horrible scene unfold. This couldn't be happening. This couldn't be Audrey Kishline—wife, mother, activist. This wasn't the Audrey Kishline who made Christmas stockings and drove her son to tennis lessons. This could not possibly be me. But it was. Painfully so.

The police arrested me in the parking lot. They handcuffed me and placed me in the back of the squad car. I could hear my friend shouting out to me as the car pulled away: "Remember my number … ." He kept repeating his number and home address so I wouldn't forget when it came time to call and write. He knew I was going away. He understood what he had done.

He saved my life.

I spent 73 days in the Clackamas County Jail in Oregon City, Oregon, one of the worst jails in the country and by far the worst jail in the state. This particular jail is what people in the system called doing "hard time." I was arrested on a mid-February afternoon in the midst of a terrible ice storm. I was kept in a holding tank, essentially a windowless cement room in the basement of the county jail. It smelled of vomit and excrement. I had never cursed before prison, but I learned the lingo in Purdy. Suddenly I found myself back in that mindset, using language that wasn't me. My vulgar language returned the moment I returned to the system. I was instantly transformed back to prisoner.

The night I was picked up, I weighed less than a hundred pounds and was still battling pneumonia. I could barely hold down what little food was in my body. I began to shiver and then I couldn't stop shaking. My lips quivered and my teeth chattered so hard I couldn't speak. Hypothermia set in. I looked around the tiny tank and saw six other women. One had open sores; another was scratching her head from lice. One inmate came in covered with blood from head to toe. There was only one filthy metal toilet that had overflowed days before my arrival. The only way to stay warm was to huddle together with my fellow inmates. I reached out and held the woman with open sores on one side and the woman covered in blood on the other. I didn't care. I was freezing. I thought I was going to die.

Once again everything had fallen apart.

The next day I was moved to another small cell where the conditions were only slightly better. This cell had a small window that was painted black. It had a tiny scratch mark made by someone else—someone who, like me, was in such immense pain, she clawed, scratched, and nicked away at the black paint, the thin layer that separated her from this hellhole and the outside world.

I didn't know if I would be sent back to Purdy or not. I waited seemingly endless days and nights to learn my fate. Since I was a convicted felon from another state, it took 30 days just to receive a hearing. After my hearing it was decided that I would have to serve 90 days or go to a treatment center, whichever came first. Every single day I hoped an opening in a treatment center would become available, but it was almost 10 weeks before one did.

I spent two months trying to work up enough courage to look through that scratch in my window, but I couldn't do it. White snow melted into fresh green spring grass. I missed another change of season. What had I done?

And still, I waited.

I received a letter from my friend explaining that he was the one who called the police. He wrote that he hoped I didn't hate him, but he felt he had no choice. He turned me in for my own good. He said he understood the conditions I was living in. His compassion and understanding were a great source of comfort. He wrote to me almost every day—I called whenever I could.

"I forgive you," I said. I told him that I understood why he did what he did. The great power and gift Sheryl had given me was never clearer than the moment I told my friend I forgave him for what he had done.

I had yet to forgive myself for anything, however, and doubted I ever could.

My children were all I could think about during those 73 days. I had ruined it all again. I wallowed in self-pity. I had no one to blame but myself.

I began to pace as I had done so many times in Purdy. I had to walk 52 laps back and forth in the main hall to walk a mile. Back and forth, back and forth, back and forth. There was nothing else to do.

I walked. I thought. I read the few books the jail had available, and then I walked some more.

The people in jail are a lot rougher than the people in prison. By the time inmates arrive in prison, they've usually had three to six months to clean up. But in jail the criminals are straight off the street. One woman in jail only left her bunk to pee. She never showered. She had greasy hair and reeked of a stench I can't possibly describe other than to say it was worse than three-day-old fish. Another woman came in who was obviously inflicted with AIDS. The lesions on her body were open and oozing. She was convinced she wrote music for the Rolling Stones. She also thought she was on the phone with President Bush, and she giggled needlessly in the middle of the night.

On my 42nd day in jail, I began to pray to God.

"God, what can I do differently? Can you show me a way? I don't know if I want to live or die. Can you give me some guidance? Can you get me through the next day? What do I need to do?"

For the first time, I heard God speak, not in words, but I felt His answer.

"You don't need to die from this. Something good can happen from this. Hang in there with me, Audrey. We're going to make it through this. I will give you meaning and purpose in your life."

Something magical happened that night in jail.

I had hope.

I made it through the next minutes, hours, nights, days, and weeks that followed—with hope. A tiny little piece of God's love came to me that night. I was frail and weak, but I gained immeasurable strength and perseverance. I felt like Job and I often thought about his story of survival and strength. I too felt I was being spiritually tested all the time. Was God bringing me to my knees to bring me closer to Him? I understood that God gives us only what we can handle, that my challenges were not necessarily worse than anybody else's; they were just my particular hurdles.

I finally turned an important corner in my spiritual journey.

I didn't know it, but I had about four weeks left until I would be released. After that night something inside me changed. I became much more open to the other women in jail and tried to be helpful to them, assisting them in writing letters and pleading their cases in an articulate way. By this time I was the old-timer, as people usually stayed in this jail for only two or three days. A week was considered a lifetime; two weeks was a death sentence. I spent a total of 73 days in the Clackamas County Jail. When I left I realized I had seen a total of four hours of daylight in all the time I spent there.

Most people released to a treatment center from jail rarely show up because their addictions drive them to go into hiding. Sadly most of those offenders end up repeating the cycle of arrest, jail, and release over and over again. The judge who released me from jail insisted I be driven directly to the treatment center by a family member. He wanted to be certain I showed up.

I came out of jail with the same clothes I was brought in wearing. They were filthy, having not been washed for nearly three months. My mother came to greet me. I was humiliated and embarrassed to see her. Brian drove me to the treatment center. It was a long, uncomfortable ride as I had no words that could possibly justify how low I had fallen. But Brian kept the conversation going. It was good to see a smile on his face again.

The treatment center was known as a last-ditch effort for people who are repeat offenders. It was a tough, intense, and confrontational program. Either inmates make it through with flying colors or they are sent back to prison for good.

The program leader ruled with an iron fist. His rules were endless dictations. The walls were covered with warnings and orders to be followed at all times. There would be no second chances. Break a rule and you would be terminated. The center refused to let anyone take medication, except aspirin. I knew I needed to be medicated, so I was panicked at the thought of not having my antianxiety medication.

Panic fed on panic.

The center was a pressure cooker of repressed tension and abject terror. It was a test of survival and strength based on brow beating and breaking a person down to build him or her back up. I thought I had been through the worst of the worst before I arrived at the treatment center. I couldn't imagine anything being harder than my 73 days in jail or my three years in prison.

I was horribly wrong.

The treatment center was far worse than prison, jail, and every nightmare I had lived throughout the previous three years. I was already broken down. How much more could they break me? I was about to find out.

I had been through alcohol treatment many times, so I thought I would just play the same game I always had, especially when it came to addressing alcohol abuse and participating in mandatory AA meetings. I'd been able to succeed with my passive-aggressive approach throughout the years. Surely I could squeak by in this hellhole. This time, however, I would pay a high price if I lost the game—a year and a half in prison.

I couldn't afford to make a single mistake. There was a big orange sign on the bathroom door that read, "If the toilet overflows, you will be terminated." The plumbing at the center was terrible, and the toilets overflowed almost daily. I lived in constant fear that I would be the person to make the toilet run over the edge. Every time I flushed, I held my breath that the water would spiral downward. Rising water in the toilet was cause for tremendous concern.

The rules in the center were harsh. I helplessly watched as another treatment center prisoner was reprimanded for inappropriately giggling. She was told to stifle any laughter or giggling for two days or she would be sent to prison. This was a serious threat, especially to this poor soul who laughed because she was nervous, not out of disrespect. Sure enough, she laughed and was removed from the program.

Another prisoner was told he could not smile—ever. Another

woman who mumbled all the time was placed on three days of silence. She talked under her breath, murmuring inaudible and incomprehensible words. On day two she accidentally bumped into someone, said, "Excuse me," and was terminated. I began to take the program seriously—more seriously than I had ever taken a treatment program before.

I was told I had to confront people twice a day. It went against every ounce of how I move through the world, but twice a day I called people out on minor infractions, like forgetting to put a folding chair back in its place after lunch, or more personal issues, such as telling someone she was a poor listener. I tried to focus on the minor things to avoid upsetting anyone, but of course, I did.

The prisoners in the center were a tough crew. Most had done hard time, and none of them cried easily, including me. But all of us learned to cry on cue. The idea was to make us cry. The staff attacked us every chance they could to cause us to break down and tap into dormant emotions. If you didn't cry, they weren't getting through. The theory was to move past the symptoms of your problems, which were being manifested in drugs and/or alcohol. They wanted to arrive at the root cause of the problems that brought on the addictions in the first place. No other program I attended ever attempted to reach that deeply into my psyche.

Being forced to confront others was a no-win situation. If I told on someone, I was a rat. If I called someone out on a personal flaw, I was a bitch. Group therapy was torture, lasting for hours each day. The room was filled with accusations and loud crying as women doubled over in pain, screaming and yelling, forced to recount unthinkable incidents from their past. Everyone was terrified of being put in "the chair" where the other inmates were ordered by the counselors to verbally attack. I always left group therapy exhausted and emotionally drained.

To survive the program I began to pray. Though I didn't have unshakable faith every day, I was beginning to build my own personal relationship with God. I felt I had hope through God, now more than ever, and I began to reread the Bible. I know I would never have made it through the treatment center program without God's help.

The treatment center forced me to become so honest that I found myself saying things that I knew might cause me to be terminated. Even so, I spoke only my truth, even if it meant I might be sent back to prison.

As I began to grow spiritually, I found an unexpected friendship with one of the female counselors at the treatment center. Maria was the one bright ray of light in an otherwise dark place. She was a soft-spoken and God-filled woman in her 40s, with dark curly hair and sparkling dark eyes. She was also a motherly, loving, and sympathetic woman. She could see right through me. God gave her that gift. The way she touched me is that she knew me, knew me like God would know my secret thoughts. I treasured every moment she spent with me, and she was not even my assigned counselor. I genuinely loved her. Her presence was a calming force in a sea of storms, and she gave me hope. Whenever she ran group therapy, I found myself reflecting instead of defending. I began to ask questions I hadn't ever considered. If God had indeed forgiven me, why did I keep returning to my pain? Why did thinking about my crime still leave me so emotionally crippled? Would I remain an emotional invalid for the rest of my life? I prayed to God all the time to provide answers, guidance, and hope.

Men and women were brought together in the center only during AA meetings and for lectures. Lectures were not generally a time of deep reflection or emotional sharing. They were meant to be uplifting and inspirational. The routine was always the same: Counselors lectured, then asked questions of the inmates, keeping careful notes on who spoke and what they said.

Most of the men in the treatment center were classified as hardened criminals. They were physically huge from doing rigorous labor and working out. Almost every male inmate had a tattoo and carved designs in his hair. The women weren't all that different. Most of us were given nicknames by our fellow inmates. Mine was the same as it was in Purdy, "The Librarian."

During one particular lecture I was called on to speak to the group. I glanced over to look into Maria's eyes for support and assurance that I could say whatever I felt. I knew it was time. I had to tell my story, honestly and from the heart.

I stood and began to speak. I told how I began MM and lied to my members. I confessed to drinking beyond the limits and guidelines I myself set and how I hid it away from everyone I knew and loved. I broke down into tears as I shared my only memory of the night I crashed. I spoke of how I awoke to discover that I had killed two people by driving drunk. I quietly whispered my confessions of my crime and all that I had lost. I shared the beautiful gift of forgiveness Sheryl had given me and talked of her incredible faith and courage. I cringed at the thought and reality of the burden and responsibility that I now realized came with her caring and thoughtful words.

I was doubled over in my chair from the pain of my admission. I was crying so hard each of the words had to be punched out one at a time. I was so intent on getting through this, I had forgotten the reason I had started speaking in the first place.

And the truth shall set you free.

Those words rang in my ears as if a loudspeaker was shoved inside my head.

When I finished a large man seated across from me began to speak. He was the kind of man who could paralyze you with a single look. He was a heavyset man with a totally shaved head and lots of tattoos up and down his muscular arms. I knew from our nightly AA meetings that this man had a violent background. He often admitted in group that he had beaten people and had often carried a gun before prison until he finally killed someone. He was filled with huge rage from one of his family members being killed by a drunk driver. Was he going to lunge at me? Could he see only the drunk driver who killed someone in his family when he looked at me? I was petrified but too exhausted to care. It took every ounce of strength I had left to raise my head high enough to see that this brute was weeping, sobbing, fighting to squeak out whatever he was trying to say:

"I forgive you, Audrey."

Those four powerful words. Words that impacted me so deeply, I was left speechless. He risked being terminated for speaking out of turn, but he took his chances anyway.

After we were dismissed, my counselor took me aside. She told me there wasn't a dry eye in the group. Counselors who hadn't been touched by anything they had heard in the center for years were weeping as hard as the inmates.

There was a moment when I knew it was God's strength that pulled me through my group confession. I also understood, for the first time since the crash, that crying is part of the healing process. Living in my pain was part of understanding remorse and forgiveness for what I had done. Speaking to the other inmates gave me the opportunity to help them see through their own suffering and guilt to healing.

My counselor stopped me for one last thought before I walked to my room. She said, "When you spoke about what you've done and how you feel, you touched people in here who have made a profession of not caring or feeling. You brought them closer to where they need to go on their own recovery journeys. Somewhere in that group is a person, if not several people, who thinks, just because they haven't killed anyone—yet—they have everything under control. They think they don't belong here. There are people you spoke to tonight who think what happened to you could never happen to them. But they're wrong. They're just in here to get through and get out so they can have their next drink, take their next hit, or commit another crime. The cycle will repeat itself until something more serious happens. And they will wind up inside for good. Or dead."

Her words could have been ripped from the pages of my life story. They cut me to my soul. I had been one of those people—once. Maybe this was God's plan? Maybe my story reached these people in a way that counselors all throughout the system had failed to over the years. Maybe my pain and regret would be a wake-up call for others before it was too late.

27 On My Own

AFTER I WAS RELEASED FROM THE TREATMENT CENTER, I understood that life would always be filled with challenges. The difference was now I was clear that my responses to life's ups and downs had to change. I just wasn't sure if I could do it.

I was still on parole for another year and a half, until August 2005. This time, though, I was allowed to go home and live with my family. It's rare that people make it through their parole without earning some kind of extension to their sentence for violating the terms of their parole. In fact two-thirds of released prisoners are rearrested within three years of release. Part of this is because there are a lot of restrictions placed on parolees. Even though I had gone through treatment, throughout the rest of my term I was required to find and keep a job; attend any group meeting my parole officer demanded, including AA; have a permanent place to live; not partake in any drug or alcohol use; and not drive.

Treatment had helped me see things more clearly. I could no longer hide from my life; I had to own up to some harsh realities and challenge myself in ways I had never tried. I had to face Brian and the kids from a whole new perspective. Sober, for starters.

Although my children had a stable upbringing, my actions most certainly took a toll on them, especially my absence during important formative years. Even though Brian was aware of my battle with alcohol in the years prior to the crash, he always said that I was a good, loving mother to the kids. We never felt they were at risk because of my drinking. Not once.

There are more than 1.5 million children in the United States who have at least one parent in prison. The system doesn't teach inmates ways to interact with their children and families after being released. Many women I met in prison lost their children to foster care, so I felt truly blessed that my family was waiting for me.

The day I caused the crash was the same day Brian's job in Chicago ended. He soon found himself buried under a mountain of debt from my legal and medical bills. He landed a job with a small software company, but it was very difficult being a single dad working 60 hours a week and dealing with his own pain, anger, and depression. Eventually the bank foreclosed on our home. As a result, he and the children were forced to live with his parents almost the entire three years I was gone. My in-laws lived close to Brian and me, so the transition was not difficult for the children. They were still able to attend the same schools and keep their friends. The consistency made life as stable as possible given the painful circumstances.

I didn't realize just how hard life would become for Brian while I was in prison. I was so lost in my personal hell that I never considered the trail of destruction I left behind when the prison gates closed. Brian was very much in love with me, but my poor choices and continual lying had deeply hurt him. He was depressed, unable to focus or gain back the confidence that made him successful in the world. He was swallowed up by our ever-growing debt, and he was a single dad raising two kids on his own. Brian had to accept lower-paying jobs to allow time to be with the kids during the years I was in Purdy. My sentence became his. He had no more choice or freedom to live in the outside world than I did locked up in prison. I will forever carry the guilt and shame for sentencing Brian along with me.

Toward the end of my prison stay, Brian and I talked about giving our relationship another try. I felt so responsible for his struggles, I gave in and told him I would try, even though I knew it was moot. After my release we didn't live together, but we decided to date. I used my parents' house as my registered address, so under the terms of my parole that had to be my residence. The children remained with Brian and his folks, which was the least disruptive choice when I came home.

I spent as much time with the children as I could in between work and my mandatory nightly AA meetings. After a couple of months, Lindsey and Samuel both asked to come live with me, and they moved into my parents' house with me. It felt so good to feel that attachment again. Brian was supportive of my spending time with the children. He believed it was helping them heal too. They began to blossom from having their mother again; so did I.

Brian started coming to visit me with the kids, spending most weekends with us at my folks' place. For a while, we became a family again. Things were going so well we decided to rent a house and move in together. Brian voiced his concerns about my stability and his fear that I couldn't stay sober. He could tell how broken down I was. Even though I was stronger as a person after treatment, I continued to falter emotionally. I wasn't equipped to handle all of the responsibility that went along with being on parole and being a wife and mother after so many years of separation from the outside world.

I hated being controlled by the system—being told what I could and couldn't do. My frustration and anger toward the parole system grew until it became another issue Brian and I fought about. Eventually our relationship slipped back to the way it was before I went to prison, and we stopped communicating. I felt muffled from sharing my real feelings and emotions. I was in a forced abstinence program, which always meant I was headed for a fall. It wasn't a question of if—only when. I had to focus on fixing myself; I couldn't adapt to all of the added responsibility of fixing us too.

Throughout my life, I had believed a hard day's work was rewarded with a few drinks at the end of the day. That is the way my father lived, and that's the way I was raised. As hard as I tried to abstain from alcohol, it was asking the impossible. I was determined not to make the same mistakes, but I did. I had no control over my desire to drink. I had no discipline to abstain from drinking.

It started with swigs of cough medicine and mouthwash, but soon the desire became bigger than those amounts could satisfy. I was afraid of the ramifications, but not enough to deter me from breaking the rules.

There was one thing I understood perfectly. If you can't find total abstinence—and many people who are recovering alcoholics don't—you cannot drive. Ever. Period. You must take every precaution necessary to ensure that what happened to me does not happen to you. I have no car, no driver's license, no availability to keys. I will never, ever drive again. I've lost that privilege for the rest of my life. The law has not mandated that. I have. It is the only way I can absolutely guarantee that what I did will never happen again. I cannot control my urge to drink, so I choose to abstain from driving. It makes my life harder, it makes traveling to work harder, and it places an enormous burden on my friends and family. But it's the right decision.

Many people go to many alcohol treatment centers and never recover. A few people turn to AA and still drink every day. I've met people with 13 DUIs, and they still drink and drive. I met a woman in prison who had three DUIs before she finally killed someone. There are a lot of high-functioning alcoholics who can drink—a lot—while most people don't even know they've been drinking. But they have and they are impaired even if they don't seem like they are. For anyone who drinks, whether a few or a few too many, there is no alternative but to leave your keys at the door. I'm not saying anything you haven't heard a thousand times before.

Three months after my release from treatment, I finally tasted my first real drink. It was on my day off, and Brian was away. I could drink and know it would be off my breath before the end of the day.

I walked to the liquor store, bought two small airplane-size bottles of wine, and I drank. I didn't binge. I didn't fall off the deep end. Most parolees slip up and are lost forever.

Not me. I was moderating.

I was lying. I was in trouble. I began to cheat on a more regular basis. I called in sick to work. I drank vodka instead of wine because it was less obvious on my breath. My shame grew with every sip.

My relationship with Brian was becoming rockier every day. I detest strife. I don't like anger between two people who love each other. I cringe at the sound of a raised voice. Although Brian rarely raised his voice, when he did I felt as if he were slapping me across the face. I had just lived three years in prison afraid every day because the guards yelled at me or raised their voices. I had to grow a thicker skin in prison to survive the abuse of the verbal lashings. But when I got out, I didn't want to have the same feelings in my own home.

I know it's normal for couples to fight from time to time—to raise their voices or yell to let their feelings out in the open. I hope it's a good thing for most people because it leads to resolving their issues and the couple grows from the experience. I never felt good about arguing. Never. The only way to deal with my growing frustration and anxiety was to get drunk. Only then could I tell Brian what was on my mind. Alcohol opened my otherwise padlocked emotional floodgates.

I had returned to the same patterns of drinking in private, lying about it, and hiding it from him. Of course, Brian knew my patterns better than anyone. He knew I was drinking again. He'd always say, "Alcohol is God's gift and the devil's brew." It is an absolute truth. I love to drink. It relaxes me and gives me a certain high. Most of the time, I feel better after I've had a few. I have more spiritual thought, my inhibitions are gone, and I feel more comfortable in my own skin.

Alcohol is the love of my life.

It's not the only thing I love. But it is something I love very much.

I kept reverting inward. The silence was deadly because I wouldn't let my emotions out for long periods of time, then suddenly I would explode. Brian and I never had screaming matches before prison. But now the kids heard us use some pretty nasty language, which they never heard growing up. They knew things were falling apart. I did nothing to shield them from the implosion that was happening within the thin walls of our rented house.

Whenever Brian went on a business trip, the time away from him gave me the opportunity to drink as much as I wanted to without worrying about what he thought. When he left—for what turned out to be the last time he left while we were together—I binged.

The next morning I called my parole officer and confessed I was drinking—excessively. I explained that I needed to move out of the house. The reconciliation with Brian wasn't working and it was placing too much stress on me. I voiced my concerns over how hard the transition back to real life was, instantly being thrust into my role as mom, readying the kids for school, and doing all of the things that came so easily before prison. Plus the conditions of my parole added responsibilities and pressure I simply wasn't emotionally or physically equipped to handle.

Somehow, in my mind, I believed that after I was released, I could slide back into my old life. Maybe I would do a little writing, take Samuel to tennis practice, carpool the kids to and from school, clean the house for Brian—all the things I took for granted. But being on parole was in itself a full-time job. The biggest surprise came when I realized I could not truly be out on my own.

My mother tells me how she has no time to enjoy life. She's always running to the grocery store, paying bills, making dinner for Frank, seeing friends, and living in her own rat race. I kept telling myself in prison that I wanted to learn to live a slower life so I could maintain that rhythm when I was on the outside. But three months into my release from treatment, I was right in the race with every other rat.

How can I make more money?

How can I afford new clothes?

How will I pay my rent?

Where can I live?

Who will hire me?

How can I save for retirement?

It was a never-ending pressure cooker, and the littlest thing would set me back. One day in a rush on my way to a mandatory drug and alcohol treatment class, I stopped off at a local bakery, ordered coffee and a muffin, and quickly dashed away so I wouldn't be late. I reached my hand into the white bakery bag, pinching off small pieces of muffin I munched along the way. I wolfed it down before realizing I had just eaten a poppy seed muffin.

A poppy seed muffin. That's all it took to set me down a one-way path of panic and absurd levels of anxiety. Poppy seeds contain an ingredient that can falsely test positive for heroin. As a felon on parole, I could be drug-tested at any time for any reason, and a positive test would send me back to Purdy. No questions asked, no acceptable excuses. Though I hadn't been tested since my release, I knew I could be on a whim in the class I was about to attend. Sure enough, I thought, this would be the day they chose me. I called my parole officer to explain I had eaten a poppy seed muffin. I needed her advice on how to handle the situation. She didn't answer the phone. I left a message as my panic kicked into high gear. I kept thinking that not only would I be branded an alcoholic, but now I was also going to be seen as a heroin addict.

I'm going back to prison for a year and a half. I can't believe this. I can't believe I'm going back. The same thought scrolled through my head like a tape that wouldn't end. I filled out the paperwork, waiting to be tested. There were three people ahead of me. Then two. Then one. Then the meeting began. They didn't test me. They just moved on. I don't know how or why it happened—perhaps it was God's will—but I was never tested.

After hearing how stressful living on my own had become, my

parole officer agreed to allow me to leave Brian on the condition I enter another work-release program until I found a place to live on my own. It's so hard for a felon to do anything, especially rent an apartment. I wanted to find a place the kids could come to visit, but none of the apartment complexes would approve my application. I was on parole as a convicted felon and had horrible credit and a new job paying minimum wage. Eventually I had no choice but to move in with my parents again. At age 45, I was like a child, unable to care for myself or nurture my own emotional needs, and I was afraid to face my fears.

Sheryl

28 What Really Killed My Family

PEOPLE HAVE ASKED ME IF I BELIEVE AUDREY'S SENTENCE was fair. The Bible says, "An eye for an eye." The consequences should be equal to the crime. If you take a life, you should have to spend your life in prison. Murder is murder. There's no other way to describe it. Someone who drinks and drives and kills two people on the road is no different from someone who robs a bank and shoots two people as he tries to escape. I believe the laws are too lenient when it comes to drinking and driving. When you sit behind the wheel of a car after you've been drinking, even if you don't intend to kill someone, you have put yourself in a position to harm someone.

To be clear, drinking is not what killed my family. It was the combination of drinking and driving. The Bible doesn't say not to drink—it teaches moderation. It also teaches there is a price to pay for overindulging. People may think it is their right to drink and drive. It is not. If they make the choice to drink and drive, they have shown they cannot be trusted to make responsible decisions. They ought to lose their licenses for the rest of their lives, and live those years remembering what they did. I know those are harsh words, but it's truthfully how I feel.

But I am not a judge, nor am I a jury.

Audrey was given her sentence and she fulfilled it.

God will be her judge.

3 Hello, Sheryl

I THOUGHT ABOUT SHERYL MANY TIMES AFTER OUR
visit. I spent much of my jail time thinking about her, wondering
how she was doing, planning how I would reach out to her. As the
end of my sentence drew near, I decided I would call after I was
released. I wanted to speak to her again. I wanted to hear her gentle
voice. I found great comfort in her kindness and virtuous heart.

One of the conditions of the civil suit settlement with
Sheryl was my commitment to write a book about the events
and my experiences before and after the crash. For most of my
incarceration, I believed I would write this book on my own. I felt
it was my duty, my obligation to Sheryl and her family. I never
wanted my story to seem more important or harder than the
nightmare Sheryl and her kids have been through. There is simply
no comparison to the magnitude of her loss. I worried all the time,
spending countless sleepless nights wondering how I could possibly
make an attempt that would feel significant enough to help ease
their pain, to soften the blow, to help them recover.

The day after I finished parole, I phoned Sheryl's attorney to see
if I could contact her. He agreed to speak to Sheryl to gauge how
she felt about my calling. I worried that she might not want to hear
from me. Perhaps she had had a change of heart. We hadn't talked
or written since our face-to-face meeting in early 2001. It was now
more than four years later, and I didn't want to inflict more pain on
Sheryl by calling. What if hearing my voice opened up old wounds?

I determined to respect her wishes, regardless of what they were: call, don't call, write a book, don't write a book. The decision was in her hands.

Her attorney responded with a message that it would be OK for me to reach out. He provided me with her phone number, which I held on to for some time before finding the strength to call.

One August afternoon in 2005, sitting in my mother's piano room, I picked up the phone. I slowly pushed each button on the receiver, wondering if I was doing the right thing. My hands were shaking, my palms sweaty from nerves. I had to redial twice because I kept hitting the wrong keys. Should I hang up? I couldn't do it. Just as I was about to smash the phone down, I heard a voice:

"Hello?"

"Is this Sheryl?"

Silence.

"This is Audrey. Audrey Kishline."

More endless, aching silence.

My heart dropped. My throat slammed shut.

"I'm so glad you called. How are you, Audrey?"

Her voice was full of the same caring love I remembered from our visit. It was light, almost musical. We talked for hours. We spoke about our children, boyfriends, jobs, family, and yes, the crash. Sheryl blew me away with her openness and willingness to bring me into her life.

The conversation turned toward writing a book together. We agreed to ask God for the strength to go through the process of revisiting the pain and reopening our maimed hearts. We wanted to share our story with others, tell them about the deaths of Danny and LaShell, the tragedy, the pain, the lessons learned, and the possibility to do anything with God's love and light. Toward the end of the conversation, Sheryl asked me if I wanted to pray.

I did. I found tremendous joy in the way Sheryl spoke of God and His power. I dropped to my knees. Sheryl prayed so beautifully.

I was incredibly moved by her every word. Unexpectedly I began to cry. I noticed my mother wiping tears from her eyes too, unaware that I could witness her emotional moment as well. I hadn't seen my mother cry since the night she told me she was leaving C.R.

Sheryl ended the call by saying, "God bless you, Audrey." Indeed I felt blessed. Very blessed.

I visited with Sheryl for the first time three months after that first call. C.R. happened to be in Seattle for a few days visiting his mother-in-law, so I called him to see if he could drive me from Seattle to Sheryl's home in Yakima. We were going to start working on the book. I was nervous about seeing her, but she welcomed me into her home like an old friend. I met Cody and some of her friends from her Bible study group. Everyone was aware of who I was, and yet they showed remarkable compassion and understanding in my presence.

The warmth with which Sheryl embraced me was puzzling at first. Here we were, two people who would otherwise never know one another, spilling our guts about everything, oddly avoiding the truth that brought us together. Through our conversations on the phone, we already knew the similarities between us. We discovered how our fathers were similar in many ways, which in turn had created issues for us both when it came to the men with whom we chose to spend our time. We understood the impact of the years we both spent in Europe as children. I felt good whenever I spoke to Sheryl because she always offered her compassion and understanding free of judgment. My guilt, my pain, and my sorrow for what I had done to this woman were ever present, but the force that drew me to her was unstoppable.

The bond I feel to Sheryl is still a mystery. But then God works in mysterious ways. There are many mornings I wake up knowing I cannot undo the choices I've made. I live with that pain every day. I try not to identify myself as only the woman who killed Danny and LaShell. Instead I live each day as someone who is trying to find what God wants me to do with my life. Sheryl has played a pivotal part in my path of discovery.

I find comfort in calling Sheryl, especially on those mornings I wake up and feel so bad about what I've done. Sometimes she feels discouraged about the things happening in her life. We've come to a place where we can lift each other's spirits. As hard as it is to explain, the rhythm of our lives seems to move on a similar plane. We have been able to talk to one another about the ebb and flow of life—the unexpected turns that come every day. Whether it's boyfriend trouble, financial stress, issues with our children, the food stamps running out, or even having a tire fixed—we are able to counsel one another because we are both single mothers just trying to get by.

As we continued to talk about our individual journeys since the crash, I often worried that somehow the details of my injuries and the agony of my incarceration would overshadow or somehow inadvertently devalue Sheryl's loss and pain. I sometimes felt she might not have articulated her true feelings to me because she was afraid of hurting me.

In time she grew comfortable enough with me to openly speak her mind, to talk about the crash. When she did, it cut me to the core. She brought up some horrible and graphic details I was unaware of until we spoke. I could see she was still in great pain. Knowing how deeply I hurt Sheryl and her family affected every ounce of my heart and soul. There were (and still are) many tears, but Sheryl always speaks with truth and conviction, standing firm in her views and perspective. Her honesty and deep love for God are what attract me to her most, and that continues to give me hope and purpose. Our lives unexpectedly intersected on Interstate 90 that icy, cold winter afternoon. I don't think anyone else could ever understand our mutual pain.

Since leaving prison I feel like I have the letter "M" written on my forehead. People look at me and all they can see is "murderer." There are days I feel useless, meaningless, like my life is not worth living. It takes every ounce of self-discipline I can muster to step out of bed in the morning, go to work at a local dry cleaners, and survive one more day—especially when all I really want to do is crawl back into bed and pull the covers over my head. But I have to work and I need to stay active. I'll do anything to keep busy so I can avoid feeling empty and insignificant.

Since my incarceration various doctors have diagnosed me with a variety of conditions including panic attacks, general anxiety disorder, obsessive-compulsive disorder, manic depression, ADHD, and of course alcoholism. Each psychiatrist I've seen has an opinion about which one of these conditions is most prominent. As a result I have been placed on a variety of medications to help balance the effects of each disorder. All the meds made me feel disconnected from my own body, as if I am not in control. Now I can afford to be on only one medication, and I'm not really sure it's effective. Is it only another addiction in my life?

I've made many mistakes in life. After my release I thought about my past a lot and desperately wished not to repeat the same patterns that brought me here. I still sometimes spend hours on my sofa, staring out the window, waiting to go to work—fearing going to work, pondering my past, worrying about my future. I think about ways to change for the better.

I think about my kids and the damage my choices have done in their young lives. They live with Brian at his mom's house in Seattle, so I don't see them very often. I also ponder my failed marriage to Brian and the new relationship I am building with my boyfriend. Although Brian and I had a separation agreement drawn up before I went to prison, we never filed it. We are still officially married, though when we both have the money, we will file for divorce.

Rebuilding my life has been much harder than I expected. The smallest decisions overwhelm me: what to wear, what birthday card to buy for someone. It sometimes takes me hours just to psych myself up enough to leave the house.

It's a horrible way to live. A person should feel like each day is a blessing and strive to make each day a miracle. I've lived most of my life never understanding that concept. My drinking and depression held me prisoner, robbing me of so many valuable moments.

Most of my family has rallied and been supportive. They have offered their forgiveness, but they carry the unfair burden placed upon them as family members. My mom has really been there for me. She doesn't understand my addiction, but she loves me unconditionally. She has helped me a number of times when I needed money, food, clothes, or medications because I have no health insurance.

My stepdad, Frank, has given me wise advice and has guided me whenever he hears about possible job leads. C.R. has written and called, but I haven't seen him much.

My brothers and sisters have helped me whenever I really needed it. They help me when they see I'm trying to help myself. I have let them down often. But when I made stupid mistakes before the crash, I would hide it. Now I'm open with them all, and this is helping them to trust me again. For a long time I didn't deserve any trust. Now with God's help, trust is the main thing I am working on. I don't ever want to lose their trust again!

After years of hiding and disconnecting, I now have a strong need to be with other people. I want to connect and build new relationships. And of course, I need to reestablish old ones too. I would like to someday be with my kids again. Lindsey grew up so fast. She was 14 when I was released from prison. In my absence she became a second mother to Samuel. It's an unfair responsibility to place on a young girl. I know Lindsey will be living on her own before I have that chance, but I hope to reconnect with Samuel while he's still young enough to want to hang out with his mom. I was overjoyed when he recently began coming to Portland for visits. I cherish our long walks and conversations. Perhaps for the first time in his life, he sees me as his mother, working hard to pull my life together, and not as that person who was always on the verge of falling apart.

In the past I've been such a poor example for my children. I spent far too many years disappointing them. Now I have made it my highest goal to live up to their expectations. Lindsey also talks to me more openly on the phone, even seeking advice about school and boyfriend issues.

Since I've been out of prison, I have worked hard to simplify my life. I have no desire to go back to my old ways. My focus has changed, due in great part to my newfound spiritual strength. My family remains concerned that I won't be able to moderate my drinking and that something horrible could happen again. My sister Tina and I remain at a distance, which I understand is best for her own recovery. My other sister, Nicole, is much more understanding. My brother Michael has found his own spiritual path and now has a better understanding that not everybody can find total abstinence. He has shown a great deal of trust in me since I've been out of prison by allowing me to rent a duplex he owns. That gesture means more to me than he could ever know. If he didn't believe I was making my best effort to have a fully functioning life, he certainly wouldn't offer me a place to live.

There are, I know, many people who have not forgiven me, and I am sure they never will. They carry their sorrow and anger every day. My heart breaks for causing them so much pain.

Perhaps most important, I also know there are many people who cannot understand why Sheryl has forgiven me. When they say, "I could never do that," I know exactly how those people feel. I am not sure I would have the ability to forgive someone if he or she killed my family. I'd be angry, filled with venom, seeking revenge.

I have often thought about how I would have felt if our roles were reversed. How would I have reacted if I were one of the victims' family? Those are the days I can truly appreciate the tremendous gift Sheryl gave me through her forgiveness. I begin to feel the strength of God and His power to forgive each of us for our sins. I'm still growing in my spiritual beliefs, and I don't understand many things. But I cling to the Bible's teaching that God loves me just the way I am.

When I'm filled with doubt, I feel Sheryl's strength and hear her words over and over in my head, "I forgive you." I have truly been forgiven—not just by her, but also by God. Although the feelings of my guilt will never completely disappear, they have dissipated through the kindness and nurturing of Sheryl and people like her.

30 Becoming Whole

I NEVER EXPECTED TO HAVE MUCH CONTACT WITH
Audrey, but as we began to talk and become acquainted, mostly
through numerous phone conversations, I realized we had a lot
in common. As hard as it may be to believe, we became friends.
When we first talked, Audrey mentioned she wanted to fulfill her
obligation to me by writing a book. I never felt she was obligated
to me in any way. She seemed deeply sincere in her desire to create
something that could help other people find their way through their
troubles, whether they were alcohol related or not. I suggested we
pray about it—that we ask God for His guidance. After many hours
of reflection, we knew that this book was something we had to do
together. It was important that both sides of our story be shared so
we could give a greater understanding to a wider variety of people
who are searching in their own lives. People who are searching for
forgiveness, hope, inspiration, meaning, purpose, answers, help—you
name it, our story pretty much covers it.

My study of the Bible kept bringing me back to a simple message.
I had to rid myself of all the bitterness, rage, and anger; I had to live
out compassion for anyone and everyone who has sinned, whether
against me or someone else. I could think of no better way to share
that message than to work together with Audrey.

It had been a little more than four years since the last time I saw
Audrey in prison. In that time I knew God had been working in my
life, and I was hoping and praying he'd been working in Audrey's life

as well. When we finally reconnected, I understood that I need not question what was going to happen or why our lives crossed in the first place. I desperately wanted to do what God wanted me to do and obey Him. I had no clue our journey would expand beyond that day I forgave Audrey.

As the process of writing this book progressed, Audrey and I spent more time together on the phone and in person. The first time she came to Yakima in August 2005 was awkward, but not hard. I knew it would be challenging for both of us, but I hoped it would also be healing. I was surprised at how easy our time together felt. Over the course of four days, I took Audrey to meet some of my closest friends. We went shopping and out to lunch. I know it sounds odd, but aside from the circumstances that had made our worlds collide, spending time with Audrey felt extremely natural.

As we got to know each other beneath the surface, I realized we had so much in common. When I was a little girl, my mom and dad thought it was cute to have me taste everyone's drinks at gatherings; Audrey and I both grew up drinking with our dads. My dad stopped drinking after his car crash. Audrey's family didn't experience that same kind of trauma—that is, of course, until the night of Audrey's crash. My family had been slapped in the face by the evil of drinking and driving and understood early on how it could change the world in a split second. I mentioned to Audrey several times that I'm certain my life would have been very different had my father not crashed his car. Who knows? Perhaps my life would have turned out similar to Audrey's if my dad hadn't stopped drinking. Maybe I would have become an alcoholic too. But by the grace of God ....

Audrey and I have spent many hours on the phone talking about everything under the sun. We've talked so long the battery on my phone died before we were done. Many of our conversations revolved around the notion of forgiveness. Audrey still has a hard time accepting that I have truly forgiven her. I have cried many times listening to her talk about her pain and guilt. I don't think her pain is bigger than mine, but I didn't murder anyone and have no idea what that kind of pain feels like. I reassure Audrey that it is OK to forgive herself. She must. I want to help guide her through that process so she can move on with her life. She can't carry her pain forever and be whole.

When Danny and LaShell died, half of me died with them. I have spent the past several years helping my sons cope and repair their lost lives. All my life I wanted to do something to help other people feel better about themselves and their lives. I didn't want to go through my own life having it be meaningless and unimportant. I want to leave this world knowing that I actually did my part to help others and didn't just talk about it. Through my friendship with Audrey, I have gained a better understanding in my own life about love, forgiveness, patience, tolerance, acceptance, and understanding.

Through this experience I have gained so much knowledge and insight into my own life. I have learned how to be a better mom for my boys, a better daughter to my parents, and a better friend to Audrey. I now have more self-love and am a stronger child of God. Through all of this, I, too, am rebuilding so I can be whole.

31 *Dateline*

Dateline NBC
September 1, 2006

Dennis Murphy: Tonight on *Dateline,* she found fame on *Oprah* and right here on *Dateline* pushing a controversial theory that people with drinking problems could drink—just a little.

Audrey, on tape from her 1994 interview: I could have one or two drinks and nothing happened.

Murphy: But something did happen.

Audrey: My two sisters were there.

Murphy: And what did they tell you?

Audrey: Two people died, Audrey. Two people died.

Murphy: Drunk and driving, she killed a young father and his 12-year-old daughter. She admitted her crime, went to prison, and then one day the mother of that 12-year-old came to visit, with a message.... Dennis Murphy with the story of two women "On the Road to Recovery."

Murphy: After all she's been through, does Audrey Kishline, founder of Moderation Management, still think her program can work?

Audrey: I have very conflicted feelings on that. Obviously it didn't work for me.

Murphy: It still exists. There are chapters around.

Audrey: The book is still on the Internet.

Murphy: Do you think people read your first book at their own peril?

Audrey: You know, whether you read my book or you walk by a 7-11 and see the bottle of wine, temptation is always out there. If you're abstinent now or a chronic alcoholic, Moderation Management won't work for you.

Murphy: Do you still believe a person can be a moderate, controlled drinker?

Audrey: As long as they're not truly an alcoholic.

Murphy: But what's that line?

Audrey: Nobody knows where it is.

32 Face to Face Again

SHERYL: I WASN'T NERVOUS MAKING THE TRIP FROM
Yakima to Portland. It was late summer 2006, and Audrey and I
were meeting to continue writing our book. We had been working
together for more than a year, but this would be only the third time
we would see each other in person during the process. The roads were
clear and the drive was one of the most scenic I've ever made. I was
looking forward to once again sitting face to face with Audrey.

The four-hour drive gave me the opportunity to spend some
quality time with my son Cody, now age 11. We spent the entire ride
talking and laughing. It was joy. It had been a long time since he and
I had taken a mother-son trip. Since the crash, life had been hard for
all three of us, but the impact seemed especially hard on Cody. Money
was often tight, so I couldn't always give my kids the extras in life.
An overnight trip to Portland was as special for us as a vacation to
Disneyland. Six years after the crash that trip represented a rebuilding
of sorts—another step in our return to normal family life.

On the way I explained to Cody I was meeting with Audrey.
They had briefly met one other time, earlier in the summer when
Audrey came to the house to visit us. Cody understood who Audrey
was, but at his age at the time, he was refreshingly free of judgment,
bitterness, and anger. I prayed those traits would remain as he grew
up. Unfazed, Cody was mostly interested in whether the hotel would
have video games for him to play and if it would be all right for him
to order room service when I had to go to my meeting.

As we drove I tried to explain to Cody that life is full of choices. We come into this world unable to choose our family, our parents, or our siblings, but we can choose our friendships. You can choose, I told him, who you talk to and who you walk away from. You can choose to have a good friendship or a bad relationship.

It has been a bit unexpected, but I truly believe that Audrey and I have the foundation to be close friends for life. If we had met under different circumstances, I am not sure we would have chosen to become friends, but that's not the case now. We've come into each other's lives for reasons that are much bigger than we could initially comprehend.

Audrey: Sheryl and I had met only a couple of times before, but this meeting was critical for our friendship. I had to face Sheryl with the truth. It was time to admit to Sheryl that I still drank—every day. I had to admit I am a daily drinker. I have a couple of glasses of wine most every night, and occasionally I drink too much. I wasn't looking forward to the moment. In prior conversations on the phone, I'd hinted to Sheryl that I still had a drinking problem. I even admitted to failing at my miserable attempts to be abstinent. However, in my quest to live an authentic life, in fairness, and in friendship, I had to tell her.

My revelation could have tested the limits of our friendship, but it didn't. Sheryl already knew the truth. She knew I still drank. Despite that ugly disclosure, she still chose to be my friend. She understands that I have an addiction, and though I didn't drink when I was in prison and most of the time on parole, there was no lack of desire. Outside the system it is a temptation every moment of every day. The want, the need, never goes away. I cannot imagine living without alcohol. Alcohol has been a part of my life since I was 16 years old. It's the only thing that makes me feel normal.

I had to tell Sheryl I still drank because the years of lying are now shedding off me, freeing me to be myself—an honest version of the person I always professed to be. I had to be honest, to live my truth. What else can I do? Lying, denying, omitting, hiding—all of those traits hadn't served me well. I had lived as two different people for so long, I was torn into fragments. All the lies were holding me back from becoming the woman I want to become.

I shouldn't have survived. But somehow I did. I had been to prison. I'd learned that living anything less than an honest life means I would have no purpose. I needed a purpose, a path, a direction.

We all do.

Sheryl: I knew Audrey drank, but I never wanted to tell her because that would have sounded like a judgment. What we needed to talk about during our phone calls had nothing to do with drinking. I knew she was home, sitting on her couch, sipping wine. She wasn't out there on the road, driving, potentially hurting someone. Audrey's drinking is for Audrey to work out on her own and through God. It may be her crutch for the rest of her life. It may be God's tool to make her struggle so He can keep her exactly where He wants her, dependent on Him. I have no way of knowing what God's plan is, but I am certain He has one for her.

Audrey: There were many times I called Sheryl after drinking a few glasses of wine. I drank before calling her so I would have enough courage to talk. I knew it was a crutch. The truth is I'm still finding courage in a bottle. Sheryl said she could tell I'd been drinking by my slurred speech. It's true; my voice lowers and I speak more openly. It's amazing that most people cannot tell—that is, unless they know me the way Sheryl knows me. Some people may think I'm weak or question after all that has happened how I can still drink—why I can't quit.

That's easy for them to say.

But ask yourself a couple of questions: What has such a strong hold on your life that if you lost it you simply could not live? If given the choice, would you choose death over living in deprivation? There are support groups for overeaters, sex addicts, drug addicts, alcoholics, and many other behaviors. Many of these groups are faith-based, encouraging people to pray to God to lose weight or to stop drinking. But a lot of people don't lose weight or stop drinking. Some will spend the rest of their lives battling their addictions.

Why would God give us those kinds of challenges?

I don't think he does.

We are all born with free will.

He didn't make any of us perfect.

There has never been a moment of doubt in my mind that Sheryl's forgiveness is real, though I haven't fully accepted it. I live with my guilt every day. It's always there. Even so, Sheryl always centers me and brings me back to a neutral place in my heart and mind. I gain huge comfort from her spiritual strength. After years of aimless doubt, I have learned from Sheryl that there is great comfort in knowing God. And though I have a more private relationship with him than Sheryl's, I now understand that his influence is a part of how I choose to live my life. He guides my actions, thoughts, and feelings.

God has been the main influence for Sheryl and me to write this book. She and I prayed often throughout the process of planning and writing it. On several occasions when I gave Sheryl the choice to continue or not, she reminded me that this project was in God's hands.

Sheryl: I have spent much of the past five years defending my decision to forgive Audrey. I hadn't been able to put my reasons into words until now. Wouldn't you want to feel the joy of being forgiven by the person you hurt and know God will forgive you the moment you ask? It has taken me a lifetime to arrive at a place where I can say these words—and mean them. I know that God doesn't grade a sin like a teacher grades a math test. He doesn't categorize sin. By God's standards, sin is sin. Compared to his perfection, it is as much a sin to kill as it is to take the Lord's name in vain. The human consequences may be quite different, but in God's eyes, we all fall short.

I have met many people who are angry and bitter. Why? Because they haven't been able to forgive someone for something and let go of their emotions. They carry a grudge that keeps building and building until there's a wall so big there is no possible way healing can begin. My healing process began the moment I was told that Danny and LaShell died. I prayed to God that he wouldn't let this tragedy be wasted. He wouldn't just take them away from me without some higher purpose. My voice hasn't always been strong, but since Danny and LaShell died, my voice has become empowered and my will remarkably resilient.

Audrey and Sheryl: In late spring 2006, the television show *Dateline NBC* asked us if together we would go back to the crash site and allow their cameras to come along to document the moment. We had talked about going back so many times, but it was never intended to be something for anyone else to witness. We imagined going there so we could cry together. We hoped and prayed that moment would bring us much-needed closure so we could truly heal.

We agreed to let *Dateline* tape the experience, but it was a mistake. Each of us was taken in separate cars, which didn't allow us to connect. On the way, the producers spoke to us individually, asking how we felt, what we were thinking, and if we were nervous to go back. Worse yet, television cameras taped our every word, our every move. In retrospect, this was not a moment we should have shared.

Several police officers escorted our caravan to the site. We were told some of the escorts were actually officers on duty the night of the crash. They were awed that we were coming there as friends.

We stood on the side of the highway, snow piled on each side, traffic whipping by, oblivious to why we were there. The noise of the passing cars and trucks was unbearable, and snow covered the crash area. We were both oddly silenced by the experience and somewhat unmoved. We stood, kicking around the snow, knowing in our guts this was not how it was supposed to be. This was the place where two innocent people died. We hugged and tried to ignore the distractions of the passing trucks, the television cameras, and the strangers surrounding us, hoping and waiting for tears or some dramatic moment that would never come—not that day.

It was only after we left that we could take it all in. In the silence as we drove away, we both thought deeply about what we had just been through.

We plan to make one final trip to the crash site. It is our hope to place a marker on the highway to remind people that two precious souls lost their lives at the hands of a drunk driver. We want the world to know and remember. We hope our lessons will inspire others to find forgiveness and to offer unconditional love.

In an instant, life for us—for the Maloys, the Davises, and the Kishlines, for all the family and friends who loved Danny and LaShell—changed forever. It tore some of us apart and brought others together. It incarcerated us and emancipated us. It brought us closer to God and it brought us to one another. We are grateful. We are blessed.

911 Calls

March 25, 2000

Washington State Patrol, Bellevue Communications Center
5:31 p.m.

Operator: State Patrol.
Tina Conn: Yes, hi. I would like to report someone who may be on the road who has been drinking.
Operator: OK, go ahead.
Tina: I talked to her; she is coming from Woodinville. She said she was going to Colville to see her dad, going toward Spokane.
Operator: So on I-90 probably?
Tina: If she could figure out where to go.
Operator: OK.
Tina: She is driving, I think, a '92 Ford four-door king cab, with duallies.
Operator: What color is it?
Tina: Brown, two-tone. Tan and brown. The main color is brown.
Operator: Where was she leaving from? Woodinville?
Tina: Yes. Woodinville.
Operator: Do you know about what time she would leave?
Tina: I think about 45 minutes to an hour ago, and she said she had been gone about a half hour.
Operator: OK. Who is the person we are trying to locate?

Tina: Her name is Audrey. Kishline.
Operator: OK.
Tina: We're just concerned about everybody else on the road if she is actually driving right now.

....

Wenatchee Communications Center, Kittitas County, Washington 6:01 p.m.

Caller: We are on I-90 going east. We just passed a pickup that pulled out going west in the eastbound lane. It's a black pickup. We were over on the eastbound lane. I don't know if it pulled off, but it pulled into a bunch of traffic.
Operator: What is your name?
Caller: ---
Operator: And your phone number?
Caller: --- . We're at exit 70.
Operator: Thank you.

Operator: 911, what are you reporting?
Caller: I would like to report a vehicle going up the wrong way on the freeway near exit 78 just about a split second ago.
Operator: Is it a black pickup?
Caller: Yeah, it was black.
Operator: OK, yeah, we have a report of that. Thanks for calling.

State DOT: I just heard you say something about a rig going the wrong way, and we wonder where he was. Was it near 70?
Operator: Yeah.
DOT: And which way was he going?
Operator: She's going eastbound in the westbound lane.
DOT: Oh, man. OK.
Operator: No, westbound in the eastbound lane.

DOT: Westbound in the eastbound lane?
Operator: Yes.
DOT: Oh my god. I thought there was something that we could do up here, but we are too far from there.
Operator: Yeah, but I've asked County to locate them. Hopefully, we can locate him.

Operator: 911, what are you reporting?
Caller: We are up Snoqualmie Pass at mile marker 68. We are in the eastbound lane heading east, and you have a guy in a big truck going right straight up there driving west in the eastbound lane.
Operator: A black pickup?
Caller: Yep.
Operator: OK, we have had it reported.

Operator: 911, what are you reporting?
Caller: Is this the State Patrol?
Operator: Yes, it is.
Caller: OK. You have a pickup heading the wrong way on the freeway.
Operator: OK, is it a black pickup?
Caller: It is dark, yeah.
Operator: OK, what marker is it at now?
Caller: We just passed mile 68; it was just a mile before that. We are going eastbound on 90.
Operator: OK.
Caller: It looked like a woman driving.
Operator: Female driver. OK, we will update them on the location.
Caller: OK. They almost had a pileup just there around the curve. It's unbelievable.
Operator: We have a unit that's on its way up and to try to contact them.
Caller: OK, I appreciate it. Thank you.

....

Operator: 911, what are you reporting?

Caller: I'm reporting a head-on collusion on Snoqualmie Pass. It just now occurred.

Operator: Where at?

Caller: We are heading west. We just crossed the summit and this truck was going in the wrong lane. Now the car is on fire. (Do you have a fire extinguisher? Be careful. There is so much traffic.)

Operator: Ma'am, what mile marker are you at?

Caller: Um, I can't see one right here. I don't know. (Are we at the summit yet?) We are on the east side of the summit.

Operator: Are you on the eastbound lane?

Caller: We are west bound. This is terrible. The whole front of the car is gone, and it is on fire.

Operator: Is anybody hurt?

Caller: Oh, I'm sure. The truck was going westbound in the eastbound lane.

Operator: Yes.

Caller: I don't know, for about a half mile. We don't know how.

Operator: Right, we had him reported. But did he wreck on the eastbound or westbound lane?

Caller: It was on the eastbound.

Operator: On the eastbound lane. OK. And you are still east of the Snoqualmie Summit?

Caller: Yes. And there are lots and lots of cars that have stopped now. There is a military …

Operator: Two cars involved?

Caller: Yes.

Operator: The black pickup and another passenger car.

Caller: Yes, a blue car.

Operator: OK.

Caller: The man with the fire extinguisher from the National

Guard …

Operator: OK, let me get this called in. Can I keep you on the line for a moment?

Operator: State Patrol, ---- speaking.
Caller: Yes, ma'am, there has been a … wreck here on I-90 at … 48 [mile marker] plus 17 $\frac{1}{2}$ [miles].
Operator: Westbound, at about 60 something?
Caller: Yeah.
Operator: What are the vehicles?
Caller: A pickup and a car.
Operator: OK, going which direction?
Caller: Uh, going east.

Operator: Sir? Do you know if anyone is injured?
Caller: Yeah, I know it looks like one guy is probably dead, and one person is not moving at all, the other one in the pickup.
Operator: The guy in the car is not moving?
Caller: The guy in the car looks dead. His head is smashed.
Operator: His head is smashed?
Caller: Yeah.
Operator: OK. Are those horns blowing from the car?
Caller: That's from the pickup.
Operator: From the pickup?
Caller: Yeah.
Operator: OK, is the person in the pickup moving?
Caller: No.
911 Operator: Neither of them are?
Caller: Nope.
Operator: OK. We will get someone on the way as soon as we can.
Caller: OK, there are tons of bystanders here, and someone with a fire extinguisher is trying to keep this thing from …
911 Operator: OK, we'll get fire and troopers on the way.

Operator: Is someone from your vehicle checking for injuries too?
Caller: I can't tell. I can just see that the whole front of this car that is on fire is gone. …There are a couple of people with fire extinguishers. There is a lot of backup now on this side, both sides of the freeway.
Operator: Has anyone gotten out the wreck vehicles yet?
Caller: I can't tell.

Operator: 911, what are you reporting?
Caller: Yes, I'm reporting a wreck on Snoqualmie Summit.
Operator: OK.
Caller: Have you had that called in yet?
Operator: Yes, do you know if there are any injuries?
Caller: Yes, definitely. Probably one dead and there is one person alive still in one of the cars in desperate need of attention.
Operator: OK, we've got a unit on the way. Thank you.

....

Caller: Hi, this is ---- from Bellevue [Communications Center]. I know that you guys are working an accident over there. Miss Kishline, the lady supposedly in the car, received a call from her sister, and her sister is on the line and wants some information. I guess the subject's name is Kishline, Audrey Kishline, and her sister is Tina Conn. Would you feel comfortable speaking with her?
Operator: Um, you can patch her through. We don't have any information. Our guys just arrived at the scene.
Bellevue: OK, I guess. Do you want me to give her your name in case?
Operator: Um, either way. I can talk to her.
Bellevue: Let me put you on hold.

Operator: This is State Patrol, may I help you?
Tina: Yes, hi. My name is Tina Conn. I'm Audrey Kishline's sister.

Operator: OK.

Tina: Apparently she has been in a major car accident.

Operator: OK, we are not aware of anyone that is involved in the accident. We have no information on the subject.

Tina: Are you on the scene?

Operator: We just arrived on scene.

Tina: OK.

Operator: I can ask an officer to give you a call when we have more information. I don't have any information on who is involved.

Tina: OK.

Operator: You have more information than I do.

Tina: OK. Do you want the information that I have?

Operator: Yes, go ahead.

Tina: My sister has been drinking. We called State Patrol to tell them about her driving and drinking, and we were very worried about her. Someone answered her cell phone a while ago and said that she had been in a head-on car accident.

Operator: OK, what is your sister's name once more?

Tina: Audrey Kishline.

Operator: OK.

Tina: She was driving a big, huge pickup with the dually wheels, the double wheels in back.

Operator: Yes.

Tina: And when I heard that she was driving …

Tina: What is the nearest hospital in this area?

Operator: They will probably be going to Harbor View, which is in Seattle. Because the airlift is in route. I don't have that information at this time because they just arrived. But that would be my guess as to where they will be going. I can ask a sergeant to give you a call as soon as they have more information for you.

Tina: OK.

Operator: You bet, we sure will.

Tina: Do you know how long?

Operator: Well, they just arrived, so it's probably going to be two to three hours would be my guess.

Tina: Before a sergeant calls me?

Operator: Yes, because they are on the scene right now and they need to block the roadway. They have to make sure everyone gets the treatment they need, and they have to investigate the scene.

Tina: OK.

Operator: But I will let them know that you would like a call as soon as he can.

Tina: Can someone just tell me if she is alive?

Operator: I do not have that information at this time. They just got there. As soon as they find something out, we will let you know.

Tina: Thank you.

Operator: Thank you very much for calling.

Acknowledgments

Sheryl
I want to thank God for all He has done and is still doing in my life.
Thank you to each and every person in my life, for without you there
is no story.

Audrey
I want to thank everyone out there who has chosen not to drive after
they have had something to drink.